Walking and Other Stories

Walking and Other Stories

By
Sally Cameron

First Published in Great Britain in 1998 by the City Literary Institute, 16, Stukely Street, London WC 2B 5LJ

A Catalogue copy for this book is available from the British Library
ISBN   0 9532537 0 8

Typesetting, layout and printing by Small Print,
The Malthouse, Llangollen. Wales Tel: 01978 861990

Foreword

Sally attended writing workshops at the City Lit from 1993 to 1996. From the beginning I was moved by her understated, focussed way of writing, her sensitivity, her wry humour and thoughtfulness. I really enjoyed having Sally in my workshops. She was committed to her writing, her responses to other people's work were always considered and helpful and she was particularly generous in sharing information about competitions and other publishing opportunities.
She is very much missed.

The City Lit is proud to be publishing this collection of her work.

Caroline Natzler

Acknowledgements

Some of these stories first appeared in other publications: *Reunion* appeared in Acclaim magazine, December/January 1994; Revenge was published in *How Maxine Learned to Love her Legs and Other Tales of Growing Up* (Editor, Sara Lefanu, Aurora Metro Press, 1995); *Walking* was published in *Short Circuits* (Editor, Melanie Silgardo, Virago 1996), and was read on BBC Radio 4, November 1996. All stories are reprinted by permission of the copyright holders.

Sally Jane Cameron 1961 – 1996

Biographical Notes

Sally was born in Leeds in 1961 and graduated in psychology and sociology from Keele University in 1983. She was diagnosed as suffering from Lupus, an autoimmune disease, but came to London in 1984 and worked as a psychiatric auxiliary nurse and later as a residential social worker in a rehabilitation project. She retired in the early 1990s due to her deteriorating health and pursued her long-held wish to write. In addition to her short stories, Sally wrote a number of articles and a chapter for a forthcoming book on psychiatric community care. She became involved in the administration of a housing co-operative in the East End of London and devoted much of her time to transforming a derelict community garden into one which is now nationally celebrated for its diversity of plants and its overall design.

After a series of illnesses borne with courage and realism, Sally died in 1996 just after her 35th birthday

Contents

Revenge

In the bluebell wood it was always cool and damp. The den, hidden by thick shrubs, was just far enough from the path to the old house to give a perfect view without ever being discovered. Passers-by often glanced at the dense, glossy leaves of the rhododendron bushes, perhaps sensing the four pairs of eyes within, but the lush green walls were reassuringly inhuman. No-one ever looked twice.

Katie was meeting the sisters to look at Margaret's breasts. The Doherty girls had extra homework so Katie waited alone in the den, lying on her back to watch the disappearing spring sunshine through the canopy of trees. She did not mind being on her own. Growing up without brothers and sisters had taught Katie the self-sufficiency of daydreams, but she was pleased by the noisy arrival of Margaret, Anne and Frances. Margaret, the eldest, was wearing a smug expression and Katie wondered if she had remembered her promise. She was eleven, a year older than Katie, and was already getting wolf-whistles. She had thick blonde hair and full, soft lips with which she had taught Katie how to kiss. Once, when Anne and Frances were not looking, they had pricked their forefingers with a razorblade stolen from Katie's father, and pressed the bloody wounds together.
'There now - you're my sister too,' Margaret had whispered. 'More of a sister than *them.*' She nodded over at where Anne and Frances were catching caterpillars in a matchbox.
'You're my blood sister,' she told Katie, her eyes shining.

Margaret threw herself down on the old tartan blanket with a sigh. Anne was on all fours, as usual, pretending to be a horse or a dog, and Katie noticed that little Frances' eyes were red.
'The bastard!' complained Margaret. 'That bloody bastard made me do my maths all over again - *and* he's given Frances another strapping.'
Frances sniffed and smiled at Katie.
'Bloody bastard!' she said proudly, rubbing her fat bottom.
Katie tutted sympathetically.
'Let's have a look,' she said, and Frances happily pulled down her

shorts to reveal four red weals across her dimpled buttocks.

'Gosh!' Katie looked at the marks. 'Did he do it on your bare skin?'

Frances nodded.

'He made me bend over the bed and pull my knickers right down.'

Margaret snorted.

'Huh! You were lucky - at least he used the soft end of the belt. I always get the buckle!'

Katie cringed but felt a little stabbing thrill deep in her stomach. Whenever she visited the sisters' house she eyed the thick belt around their father's ample waist. Mr Doherty often appeared in Katie's daydreams, wielding his belt and grabbing at her pants, before her own father emerged at the last minute to rescue her.

'Well,' said Margaret, 'what shall we do tonight?'

Katie wondered if she was pretending to have forgotten. Margaret liked to keep people in suspense. Anne was jumping around on her hands and knees, whinnying and pawing the ground.

'Look at me! I'm a Palomino.'

Margaret aimed a vicious kick at her flank.

'For God's sake - cut that out will you!' She tried to grab her sister's hair but Anne was already galloping off into the undergrowth.

'She's driving me up the bloody wall,' sighed Margaret, lying down and stretching her arms over her head so that her T-shirt rose temptingly above her cut-off jeans.

'Oh I'm so *bored*,' she moaned. 'What shall we do?'

Katie waited for a moment, trying not to sound too eager.

'I thought you were going to show us, Margaret,' she ventured.

Margaret raised her head in feigned innocence.

'Show you what?'

Frances giggled.

'You know,' Katie was embarrassed. 'Your - your bust.'

Margaret sighed wearily.

'Oh yes - I'd forgotten. We-ell, I s'pose so.' She sat up, brushed her hair back and smiled at Katie. 'Mum's going to buy me a bra next week.'

Katie breathed admiration.

'Well then - ' Margaret sat forward on her knees, forced back her shoulders and looked down, pulling the front of her baggy white T-shirt tight over the points of her breasts. Then she cupped one mound gently underneath.

'See? What do you think?'

Katie could barely conceal her disappointment.

'Gosh,' she managed, before her impatience got the better of her. 'Well, you can't see that much actually. I thought - I thought you were going to, well, you know - show us properly.'

'I've seen!' sang Frances. 'I've seen her in the bath!'

Margaret gave her a withering look and then glanced slyly at Katie.

'Well,' she said. 'Okay, but don't tell anyone.'

Katie shook her head vehemently, and when Margaret pulled up her T-shirt she almost gasped at the transformation, not at the soft curves which she had already felt, pressed close to Margaret as they kissed, but at the new, swollen pink nipples. Katie was just about to think of an excuse for getting rid of Frances when there was a tumultuous crashing of bracken and Anne fell panting onto the blanket. 'Quick!' she cried breathlessly. 'Come quick!'

Frances slipped her hand into Katie's as they ran through the woods, her short, fat legs struggling to keep up with the older girls and dragging Katie back.

'Come on!' Katie hissed, but already Margaret and Anne had stopped far ahead and were peeping through the trees into the clearing beyond. Margaret had one hand over her mouth as if she was going to be sick.

'Oh Jesus!' she whispered as Katie reached them. 'Will you look at that!'

In the middle of the glade stood two boys, each with a handful of stones which they were hurling at the trunk of an oak tree. On the trunk was nailed a baby thrush, its wings pinned in crucifixion. Its head twisted and jerked as it let out shrill, rhythmic cries. Anne hung on her elder sister's arm.

'Come on!' she whispered urgently. 'Do something!'

But Margaret held her back.

'Wait!'

Anne pulled at Katie's arm.

'Come on! There's four of us - come on, Katie.'

Katie hesitated and looked at Margaret who was peering at the boys.

'No, wait will you. Look - they're going.'

The boys, growing bored now that the thrush had stopped moving, began to wander off towards the big house. One of them turned, aimed a last stone at the bird and whooped with delight.
'Skill! Did you see that?' He jumped on to the other boy's back and wrestled him to the ground. They rolled around, squashing the bluebells for a while, and then the bigger boy jumped up.
'Race you to the gate!'

The girls crept quietly out of the undergrowth. Slowly they approached the tree in single file, Margaret leading, but they stopped some feet away from where the bird hung, its head bent on its chest.
'Is it dead?' whispered Anne. 'Have they killed it?'
Margaret took a step closer and then looked around her for a stick. Tentatively she leaned forward and prodded the thrush very gently. It managed to raise its scrawny head and Katie thought the bird looked straight at her before giving a choked cough. Blood poured out of its beak. Frances screamed, and Margaret turned her head away.
'Oh come on,' she said hurriedly. 'Let's go - it's had it anyway.'

In bed that night Katie kept seeing the thrush's beady eyes. She wished that they had killed it. That would have been the right thing to do, what you were supposed to do with animals in pain. Once she had watched her father kill a sick rabbit that they had seen in the countryside. He had insisted on stopping the car, and told Katie not to look, but she could not help peeping as he raised his big shoe over the quivering animal. She had even glanced at the body afterwards, its red and white entrails oozing out of the split skin like a piece of squashed fruit and she had watched her father clean his shoe on a clump of grass, streaking the ground with dark blood. Katie wondered if the thrush was still alive. In her mind she took her father back to the glade where he knocked the boys' heads together and rescued the little bird, giving it to Katie for a pet.

'I've got a plan,' Margaret told them. 'I know how we're going to get those bloody bastards and make them sorry.'
They were sitting in the den trying to roast potatoes on a tiny fire.

'Not both of them at once - but we can get one of them easy,' explained Margaret. Katie prodded a potato hopefully, but it was still as hard as it had been in the kitchen. Privately she was rather scared by the idea of avenging the murder of the thrush, but Anne and Frances were excited.

'Oh yes!' shrieked Anne, rearing on hind legs. 'Four on to one - that'll show them. How, Mags, how?'

'Sshh.' Margaret put a finger on her lips and they all listened to the rapid footsteps on the gravel path. Four pairs of eyes watched, for the third time that evening, as the bigger boy raced past the den, shortly followed by his panting, red-haired friend. As they disappeared Margaret turned to the others with a superior smile.

'You see that?' she said. 'Now listen carefully.'

Katie and Frances sat in the den grasping one end of the rusty wire. Katie could not see Margaret and Anne but frequent jerks of the wire reassured her that they were still at the other end, hidden behind the bushes on the opposite side of the path. Katie ran through Margaret's instructions again, wishing that she had not been lumbered with little Frances who was sure to forget what to do, or lose her nerve, or giggle at the wrong moment.

'What are we going to do to him?' whispered Frances. 'When we've got him - what are we going to do?'

'Sshh - punish him,' replied Katie vaguely, keeping her eyes on the path.

'Will we kill him?' Frances' eyes were wide. 'Kill him dead, Katie?'

Katie wished that Frances was not there. She could feel a tingling between her legs and squeezed her thighs together hard.

'Oh no,' she told the smaller girl. 'Nothing like that - we're just going to make him sorry.'

It had begun to grow dark and Katie had cramp. She knew her mother would be starting to worry and she thought of shouting to Margaret and Anne, telling them to call the whole thing off. She rubbed her leg and brushed the midges from her hair and then, just as she was about to tell Frances to drop the wire, she heard the frantic footsteps. Katie's heart started to thump. She looked back at Frances' round eyes and tightened the grip of both her hands on the wire.

'Ready?' she whispered. 'Remember, don't pull until you hear Margaret.'

Frances nodded gravely. Katie turned back to the path and saw the big boy hurtling towards them. He skidded briefly around the bend but quickly regained his balance and shot past. He was out of sight by the time the smaller boy came running up behind in red-faced pursuit. Katie just had time for a moment's panic, to think that Margaret had surely left it too late, when she heard the shout and pulled as hard as she could, the wire cutting into her hands as she fell backwards over little Frances.

She did not see the boy smash to the ground with his animal yelp and she could hardly believe it had worked. Then she heard Margaret calling her name, and she was running to where the sisters stood over the body. He was only momentarily stunned and it was not long before he recovered, kicking and lashing out with his arms.

'Get a leg each!' cried Margaret. 'Sit on his chest, Anne!'

Anne was barking madly like a boisterous puppy and she leapt onto the boy's chest, growling enthusiastically. Margaret deftly slipped a length of wire around the boy's throat and pulled it tight so that his head jerked back suddenly with a rasping little cry.

'Now don't move, you bastard, or I'll strangle you!' Margaret tweaked the wire in demonstration and the boy stopped his struggling and lay breathing hard.

'Right, girls. Get him in the den.'

With Margaret holding the wire around his neck they lifted him easily, for he was a skinny boy, not much bigger than Katie. As they laid him on the floor of the den they heard the sound of footsteps coming back up the path.

'Mickey! C'mon - where are you? Aw, Mickey, c'mon mate!'

Margaret tightened the wire around Mickey's neck.

'Not a word!' she hissed. 'One word and you've had it.'

Silently they watched the big boy march up the path, kicking at the gravel.

'Mickeee!'

He turned and stared into the undergrowth for a moment and Katie's heart seemed to stop as he screwed up his eyes. But then he sauntered off with a shrug, hands in his pockets, and his shouts faded into the distance.

'Okay,' said Margaret. 'Okay, *Mickey.*' She savoured his name slowly. The boy's face was pale beneath his freckles and his voice came out in a squeak.

'L-let me go.'

'Let me go - what?' demanded Margaret.

'Please,' squeaked Mickey. 'Let me go *please.*'

'No!' Margaret burst out laughing and winked at Katie. 'Not until we've finished with you, you bastard. You're going to be really sorry.'

'Beat him!' squealed Frances. 'Beat him like Dad does!'

'Yeah!' Anne shouted. 'You're going to be sorry, you bird murderer!' She bared her teeth and gave a low growl before dropping on to all fours and sniffing at the bottom of the boy's trousers.

'Fucking hell!' cried Mickey, wriggling away from Anne's snuffling head. 'What's up with *her?*' He looked around wildly.

'Oh, she thinks she's a rottweiller,' Margaret explained. 'Unfortunately for you,' she added casually as Anne suddenly snarled and sank her teeth into Mickey's ankle, hanging on with clenched jaws as the boy shook his leg and yelled.

'For God's sake! It weren't me! It weren't - honest - it were Pete, not me.'

'Huh.' Margaret sneered. 'We saw you, actually. Actually we all saw you doing it - so shut your face.' She squeezed the wire again and Mickey choked. Margaret smiled.

'Trousers, Katie,' she ordered.

'Nooo!' Mickey resumed his struggling but Margaret pulled the wire tighter.

'Silence, bastard!'

Katie could see red lines on the boy's neck. She took a deep breath and, crouching at Mickey's side, bent over the flies of his jeans, struggling with the button and sliding down the zip. She glanced up at the boy's face which was beginning to flush angrily to the roots of his ginger hair. Slowly Katie eased over his thin hips, sniffing the unfamiliar, slightly rancid smell, and then pulled to expose his hairless thighs. Mickey looked as though he were about to cry. He closed his eyes as the girls regarded the stains on his blue nylon underpants.

'Pants, Katie,' said Margaret.

The boy groaned and Katie hesitated, eyeing the bulge between his legs. At home, by the bathroom door, she had often tried to peep in at her father, but she had only ever seen his head and shoulders over the top of the bath. Suddenly Katie no longer wanted to know, but Margaret was fixing her with an imperious glare. To back out now would mean weeks of retribution. She adjusted her position and, kneeling, took a firm hold of each side of the nylon pants. She looked up at Margaret.

'Ready?' she managed.

Margaret nodded.

'Get 'em off!' roared Anne.

Katie closed her eyes and clumsily ripped down the pants, feeling her hand brush against something sickeningly soft and snaky. There was a loud scream behind her and she turned to see Margaret's face crumpling. Margaret screamed again, and then Anne screamed too, and Frances shrieked, and as Katie looked down the sisters shot out of the den and charged off through the woods. As the boy began to move Katie stopped staring and somehow remembered how to work her jellied legs. Then she threw herself after the sisters, stumbling and ripping her clothes on branches as she tore through the trees.

'Wait!' she heard herself crying. 'Wait for meee!'

When Katie reached the big gates the girls were slumped in a heap against the wall, panting. Katie fell onto Margaret, breathing in her sweet warmth.

'Yuk!' said Margaret. 'Oh yuk, that was really disgusting!'

'Yak!' agreed Frances. 'Bleeahh!'

When Katie found enough breath to speak she turned to Margaret.

'Are they - are they all like that?'

'Like what?' Margaret sounded angry but Katie had to know.

'You know - like - like worms and boils and guts leaking out and . . .'

'Shut up!' Margaret put her fingers in her ears. 'Oh yuk! I feel really sick.' She pushed Katie roughly away and lay staring silently at the sky.

Anne trotted up. 'Look at me - I'm a stallion with a great big - '

'Shut up!' Margaret grabbed Anne by the hair and punched her hard. Then she stalked off down the road. Katie knew it was no good trying to follow her. No-one could speak to Margaret when she was in one of her moods.

'C'mon,' she said to the younger girls. 'You'd better go home.'

She gave them a little push in the direction of Margaret's retreating figure. 'See you tomorrow.'

For a moment Katie paused and looked at her watch. She was going to have to think of a good excuse to tell her father. Katie glanced back at the dark trees. She did not think she would tell him about Mickey. Katie did not want to think about Mickey ever again.

Real Life

I was driving over to Caro's, snuffling into my tissue and checking in the rear-view mirror for stray mascara. It was the first time my daughter, Lizzie, had stayed overnight with Siobhan and I knew I should be looking forward to my evening of freedom, but when she kissed me goodbye and scampered up to Siobhan's bedroom with her suitcase full of Barbie dolls, I just knew I was going to go wet.

I go wet every time Lizzie grows up a bit more, leaves me for new adventures, each time I lose a bit more baby. That's one of the things about being a single mum, you spend all your time worrying about the future until it's too late. You've missed the moment and your child will never be the same again.

'What are you going to do while I'm at Siobhan's?' Lizzie had asked the previous day. 'Will you be lonely?'
My daughter, at nine, can never slip fully into the selfishness of childhood for long.
Sometimes I think we worry about each other twice as much as normal, perhaps to compensate for the fact that Ted seems not to worry about either of us at all.
'I'm going to Caro's,' I told her.
For a moment she bit her lip, wanting to come too. Lizzie loves Caro, whom she has known all her life and Caro, surprisingly, has remained constantly adoring.
'You see, you're going to stay with your friend and I'm going to stay with my friend,' I told her. 'That's fair isn't it?'
Lizzie smiled.
'Don't smoke will you, at Caro's?' she said.
I'd given up for six months, but Lizzie was well aware of Caro's influence. I shook my head.
'And tell Caro to stop smoking too.'

I joined the heavy traffic into London, wondering if Lizzie would get homesick during the night, and hoping Siobhan's mother wouldn't let the girls go out on their own. Siobhan, I knew, was more daring than

Lizzie, less scared, and there was something in her perfect little smiling face that I didn't quite trust. I didn't like the way she teased Lizzie about being fatherless and I didn't like the way the two of them giggled behind my back, but I told myself that all nine-year-old girls were the same. Had I the choice, I would never have picked Siobhan to be Lizzie's best friend, but at the same time I kicked myself for my judgmental suspicions. It was unlikely, I smiled to myself, that my own mother would have blessed my friendship with Caro.

It was hot and muggy but the roads were clearer than usual, the rich having left London for August, and I arrived at Caro's flat only half-an-hour late. I hammered on the door.

'Piss off you slag!' she shouted through the open kitchen window. 'I said seven o'clock.'

Then she flung open the door, grabbed my bag and grinned the grin I've got on a hundred photos, the one she says looks like she's slept all night with a coat hanger in her mouth.

'Good haircut! How was the journey? How's Lizzie? Gin?'

Caro and I never kiss each other. She patted my new bob and turned me around to admire the back view before filling tall glasses with ice and pouring long gin-and-tonics as I sat at the kitchen table, telling her about Lizzie, and Siobhan.

I was well into my second gin by the time I'd finished. Caro sucked her teeth.

'She's a nasty little piece of work,' she agreed, 'but not dangerous. It'll all be over in a couple of months - Lizzie'll be heartbroken for about an hour, and then she'll have a new best friend and she won't be any the worse for wear. She'll have drunk a glass of Siobhan's mother's sherry, played with matches and been sick on a cigarette - she has to do it sometime.'

Caro reached for a packet of cigarettes and extracted a pure white tube with a gold band.

'St. Moritz!' I laughed 'Have you gone pretentious or what!'

She lit up and drew a long lungful, wincing slightly.

'Painful lungs,' she told me. 'Menthol's the only thing that doesn't make me choke.'

She didn't look ill. Her eyes were as bright as ever and I couldn't tell how much weight she'd lost under her baggy T-shirt.

'How are you?' I asked.

She stretched out her long brown legs and examined her scarlet toenails.

'Good tan, don't you think?' she said

I nodded.

'I bought it in a bottle in Boots,' she said. '£3.99. Have you seen Ted?'

I told her all about Ted as she cooked us pasta with little strips of smoked salmon and crème fraiche. She had opened a bottle of white wine and I knew I was beginning to babble, but it didn't matter with Caro. Caro has a way of listening, of absorbing, of feeling other peoples' pain.

'Bastard,' she growled occasionally as I talked and then, over dinner, we began to laugh as she plotted a course of outrageous revenge. By the time we had finished Ted really didn't seem to matter anymore.

'Can I phone Lizzie?' I asked her. 'Just to make sure she's okay.'

Caro grinned at me.

'Alright Miss Neurotic, but try not to slur your words or you'll never be allowed here on your own again.'

I could hear Siobhan's mother calling Lizzie for ages before she came to the phone.

'Mum? What is it?'

'Nothing, I just wondered how you were.'

'Mum, I'm *fine*. Can I go now?'

Caro blew a kiss and pointed at the phone.

'Caro sends you her love.'

'Oh - can I speak to her?'

I passed the phone and heard my daughter's loud chatter as Caro held the receiver slightly away from her ear.

'Yes - yes - no - absolutely not - I promise - yes - I love you too - bye.'

She raised her eyebrows at me.

'The child is a tyrant,' she said. 'She's just told me that if I let you smoke she's going to live at Siobhan's forever.'

I pointed at her cigarettes.

'Gis one!'

We giggled and she threw me the packet.

'So do you want to hit the town?' asked Caro as we lay end-to-end on her enormous sofa.
'Actually I don't think I can move,' I laughed.
'Oh good,' she said. 'I'm a real party bore these days - I get so tired, you know.'
It was a big admission for Caro. I jumped at the knock at the door and Caro groaned melodramatically.
'But they just can't keep away!' she cried.
'Who's that,' I asked, watching her expression change to mischievous delight. 'Oh God, not a man!'
Caro snorted and staggered off the sofa.
'Straight faces,' she instructed. 'My luscious neighbour, no doubt.'

I snatched a glance at the mirror as she went to open the door, thinking that I looked middle-aged.
'Chrissy - Graham.'
He was a big man, not Caro's usual type, solid like a rugby player. He had sandy hair and a bland sort of face with an unfinished quality about it. He smiled at me, showing a set of very small teeth of which there appeared to more than the usual number.
'Pleased to meet you, Chrissy,' he said. 'Listen, girls, I'm having some friends round for a drink, bit of a party. It'll be a good crack - Polish vodka in the freezer - why not come round?'
Caro sat down in the armchair opposite him and crossed her bare legs slowly in front of her. I watched his eyes check the bottom of her mini-skirt.
'Chrissy and I are having a girls' night in, Graham,' said Caro.
'Doing what?' asked Graham.
'Oh, you know, talking about girls' things,' said Caro lighting a cigarette.
Graham laughed.
'What girls' things?' he persisted. 'What do you girls talk about when you get together?'
'Men,' said Caro, smiling sweetly at him.
Graham flushed slightly.
'Okay, babe,' he said. 'I'll leave you to it. Pop round if you run out of

things to say.'
Caro kept on smiling.
'Oh we will,' she said.
He winked at me.
'Maybe see you later,' he said. 'I'll see myself out.'

We waited until the front door clicked shut before collapsing onto the floor.
'He called you babe!' I shrieked. 'Caro - you've been having an affair with a man who calls you babe! I don't believe it!'
'What do you think?' she asked.
I screwed up my nose.
'Not my type. Nice shoulders, I suppose, but a bit of a slime-ball.'
'Charming,' said Caro. 'The word is charming.'
I raised my eyebrows. She collapsed into giggles again.
'Oh Christ,' she sighed. 'Why, oh why? Shall I open some more wine?'
'Can I have mine intravenously? I don't think I'm capable of manoeuvring the glass to my lips. I thought you were supposed to be cutting down anyway.'
'I am,' said Caro. 'Fourteen units, the recommended intake for women. I'll just tell the doctor I thought it was a daily allowance.'
She brought in another bottle and the corkscrew.
'Is he good in bed?'
She studied the label on the wine.
'Eleven per cent. Gnat's piss!'
'Well?'
'You know, Chrissy,' she said, twisting the corkscrew slowly into the bottle. 'I was thinking about all the times we used to chase men, play them at their own game, up front, hands down their pants before they'd even bought you a drink - '
'Ahem - *your* hand down their pants if you don't mind!'
'Oh, come on, Chrissy, you were just as bad, slappers together - all out to get what we thought we wanted.'
She looked at me.
'But you know there was something wrong - I don't mean I didn't want it - it's just that somehow I began to realise that it wasn't a natural role. I didn't want to be the assertive one any more, the

chaser. I wanted to be chased. I wanted to slouch about in a ragged, floral frock, looking like something out of a Tennessee Williams play, and I wanted to be picked up, and carried off, and thrown on the bed.'

'Thrown?'

'You know, have you ever been picked up and thrown onto the bed?'

'Caro - that's not Tennessee Williams - that's pure soap opera.'

'Chrissy, my life *is* a bloody soap opera.'

Caro pulled the corkscrew violently from the bottle and filled our glasses.

'It always has been a soap opera because I don't know how to lead a real life. I was brought up on Instant Whip and the Famous Five. Graham's not *real*. He calls me babe and he struts in here like Marlon Brando, and *he threw me on the bed!*'

I spluttered into my wine.

'Oh you're not serious! He didn't!'

Caro had stopped smiling.

'He did. He picked me up and carried me in his arms to the bedroom and he threw me on the bed - and I thought 'this has never happened to me before'. Why has this never happened to me before? All the men I've had, and not one of them has ever picked me up and thrown me on the bed.'

I realised suddenly that Caro must be as drunk as me.

'No-one's ever thrown me on the bed either,' I said. 'What was it like?'

She stared at me.

'Was it good?'

Caro burst out laughing.

'Yes,' she said. 'Marvellous. It was a marvellous *idea*. But my mind just wasn't on the job. All I could think of was 'Just wait till I tell Chrissy!'

'So,' I said. 'Are we going to the party?'

We stood in front of Caro's wide mirror, applying lipstick.

'Are we mad?' I asked her.

'Yes,' she said. 'Just like old times.'

Before Caro got ill, before I had Lizzie, we used to go out every night. I was feeling the same tingling excitement as we shared a cigarette and Caro's mascara. We used to dance a lot. Caro and I would dance to anything, anywhere. Once, in a guest-house bathroom in Brighton, we had danced to the sound of a dripping tap.

Caro started back-combing my hair.
'What happened to Dominic?' I asked her.
'Married,' she replied. 'In May. I wasn't invited. A pity really, I kind of wanted to stand at the back of the church in a Joan Collins veil and put the shits up him.'
'When did you last see him?'
'A couple of months before. He turned up one night all maudlin and ended up staying. Strange.'
She stopped combing my hair and looked at me in the mirror.
'He was on a guilt-trip, of course. They make these daft rules for themselves, don't they - so we didn't fuck. But he let me do everything else-like he was trying to pretend to save his virginity for his bride or something.'
She sneered.
'And then he fell asleep with me holding him, and every time I tried to let go, to move away, he twitched and jerked and cried like a baby in his sleep, so I held him all night like his bloody mother or something.'
It was hard to imagine. Caro hated even to share her bed after sex, let alone be in someone's arms all night.
'Yeah like his fucking mother and his fucking whore all in one night - that's what they say though isn't it - the psychoanalysts - mother, Madonna, whore. Shame I never get to be the Madonna.'
She smiled at me in the mirror and patted my hair.
'Ready?'
'I'm glad I'm not a man, Caro,' I said. 'You observe them like insects, dissect them afterwards.'
'Better than eating them,' she replied. 'Shall we go?'

As we walked round to Graham's flat I remember that I was no longer remembering. Lizzie, Ted, the bills, my dreary job and the hole in my exhaust were suddenly, for the first time in weeks, not forgotten but secondary. I can remember the warm evening breeze blowing up my skirt and the lights in the houses looking exciting, the possibility of other peoples' lives changing my own.

Graham opened the door holding a screwdriver and kissed Caro briefly on the cheek.

'Sound system's just gone off,' he told us. 'Go in and get yourselves a drink.'

I followed Caro into the hot, smoky flat, edging past a group of tartan-shirted men in the hallway and into the crowded kitchen.

'Hello boys,' said Caro. 'Where's the vodka?'

I saw a pretty blonde girl give her a look of distaste but one of the men passed her a bottle of vodka and a glass.

'And one for my friend,' said Caro.

She handed me a huge glass and poured three inches of vodka into it.

'Any mixers?' I asked.

'Lightweight!' she whispered into my ear. 'Get it down you!'

'And what's your name?' slurred a man in an orange silk shirt, offering me a cigarette.

'Chrissy.'

He had black curly hair which looked permed, and skin that shone sweatily. I took a gulp of vodka and choked.

'Steady on, babe.'

He patted my back and let his hand rest over my bra strap. My eyes were watering and I could feel the vodka burning somewhere around the top of my nose.

'Alex,' he said, massaging me between the shoulderblades. 'Hey, guys, this is Chrissy - Caro's friend.'

There was a muffled snigger behind me which reminded me suddenly of Siobhan. I looked round for Caro but she had disappeared. I spotted a carton of orange juice on the table, extracted myself from Alex's arm and topped up my glass. I took a long drink and wiped under my eyes.

'Better now?' said Alex, coming up behind me and kneading me roughly in the back.

'Yes thanks,' I said. 'You can stop the First Aid now.'

I took two steps sideways and ended up sandwiched against the wall. It was so hot I could hardly breath.

'Any friend of Caro's is a friend of mine,' said Alex. He lit my cigarette. 'Do you live far?'

'Miles away,' I said. 'Excuse me - I must powder my nose.'

I pushed past the group of tartan shirts in the hall, found the bathroom and locked myself in. I looked in the mirror, wishing I had brought some make-up with me, and repaired my smudged eyes with a piece of toilet paper. The naked lightbulb in the white bathroom made me look like a gargoyle. Holding on to the sink I realised that I was much too drunk. The Rolling Stones suddenly blared out of the living-room. Caro would be dancing now, and I thought I would probably ask her for the keys and go back to her flat, to bed. I wondered if she would come with me. We always used to say the best things about a party happened before and afterwards. Even if I left now, on my own, I knew I would get to live the party again, drinking coffee on Caro's bed tomorrow morning.

I opened the bathroom door and walked straight into Alex.
'Not so fast now, babe,' he said pushing me back in. 'I was wondering where you'd got to.'
His arms came round me and he kicked the door shut behind him, pinning me against the sink.
'Now, babe, what about a little kiss?'
I strained against him but he pushed me backwards so the edge of the sink bit into my back.
'Come on now, I thought you were a friend of Caro's - Graham told me she had a friend for me.'
He pushed his knee between my legs and forced me further back. I felt like my back was going to break and all I could think about were insects, pinned like a specimen under the glare of the white light. Not even a butterfly, I was caught like an ugly moth. I screamed.

Graham looked irritated when he opened the door.
'What the hell's going on?' he demanded.
Alex let go of me and turned to the toilet, unzipping his flies.
'She doesn't like me, Graham,' he smirked, letting out a noisy stream of urine into the bowl.
Graham ignored me.
'Why don't you look after Caro for me then,' he said. 'She's not too fussy.'

Alex looked over his shoulder.

'Generous of you, mate.'

'Got my responsibilities,' said Graham. He winked at Alex. 'Remember, a dog's not just for Christmas.'

He turned to go but Caro was standing at the door.

'Talk of the devil,' said Graham smiling.

Caro's look of contempt was only slightly spoilt by the lipstick on her teeth. One of the tartan shirts stumbled into the bathroom with a bottle of vodka.

'Okay, which one's Caro?' he grinned. 'The one that fucks like a rabbit?'

Caro took my arm.

'It seems you've messed up my rental service, Graham,' she said. 'Let me know when you've sorted out a rota.'

We left.

'Bastard!' spat Caro as we walked home.

My head was throbbing. Suddenly she sat down on a low wall and pulled me next to her.

'Let's go back.'

'What?'

She nodded at the front door of a terraced house. On the doorstep were four empty milk bottles.

'Through his window.'

She skipped up the path and picked up a bottle, then another.

'Better take two - my aim's not as good as it used to be.'

Under the streetlights her eyes were shining.

'Wait here for me if you want.'

'Caro,' I said. 'He doesn't even care about you. He'd call the police.'

'So?'

'I'm too drunk to come and bail you out.'

She looked at me for a long time. Then, very carefully, she placed the bottles on the wall. I'd never seen her do that before. I'd seen her throw bottles through windows, off roof-tops, at cars, at men and at nothing at all, but I'd never seen her change her mind.

'Do you think I'm growing up?' she said.

We got up very late the next day.

'I'm giving up men,' said Caro over breakfast of bacon sandwiches and paracetamol. 'Bad for my health.'

She looked different without make-up, tired and pale. Caro looked ill. I wondered how she had looked in hospital and why it was that she always refused visitors when her health failed her. That morning I'd seen her tipping pills from many different bottles, more than I'd ever seen before.

'Tell me about your holiday,' I said.

First thing in the morning, with her mask off and her defences destroyed by a hangover, was the nearest you could ever get to Caro.

'Holiday?' she said. 'Oh - you mean my convalescence trip?' she laughed. 'Enlightening,' she said sarcastically. 'No, seriously, it was good for me. I was just out of hospital, feeling pretty shit and I needed peace and quiet, with no-one fussing over me, asking me how I was, Cornwall seemed like a good option - rolling waves, peaceful sunsets, birds, that sort of thing.'

She reached for her cigarettes. I pulled them away and she stuck her tongue out at me and continued.

'Yeah - it was good for me - it made me realise that I'm not normal, never will be, because the sunsets for me weren't peaceful at all. They looked chaotic. At a bird sanctuary I tried to watch ravens being sinister and the puffins being cute, but I couldn't take my eyes off the people, the couples, identically dressed with their children in sensible shoes and I listened to the fathers' silence and the mothers telling the kids what not to do, and sneered, Chrissy, I *sneered*. And I thought to myself, just who do you think you are, to have contempt for real life.'

She touched my arm.

'Do you think I'm sad?' she asked.

'Do you feel sad?'

'No, I mean do you think I'm a sad individual?'

'Of course not,' I said. 'No-one would ever think that - you're too much fun.'

Caro nodded slowly.

'Fun,' she said. 'Fun's alright when you're young. It all changes though, doesn't it? Suddenly. One minute you're fun and the next you're a dog.'

'Oh come on!' I said. 'You're not going to take any notice of that bastard are you?'

'No,' she said. 'It's not just that. It's just this morning I woke up with the feeling that the carnival had been rained off.'

'Come back with me,' I said. 'Stay for a few days - Lizzie'll love it.'

Caro shook her head.

'Thanks, Chrissy, no.'

'Are you sure?'

'Yeah - thanks - and Chrissy, thanks for last night.'

Lizzie squeezed me so hard I thought I was going to be sick.

'Mummy you look really rough.'

She chatted happily all the way home, telling me about Siobhan's dog, Siobhan's brother's bike, the horrid shepherd's pie that Siobhan's mother had cooked, and the noises Siobhan's father made in the bathroom.

'What did you do Mummy?'

'Oh, you know,' I said vaguely. 'Chatted, ate a lovely meal, drank some wine.'

Even though I wasn't lying I felt guilty.

'Where did you go this morning?' I asked her. 'Siobhan's mother said you'd gone out.'

Lizzie looked out of the car window.

'Oh, just out.'

'Out where?'

We stopped at traffic lights and I looked over, but she was staring intently away.

'Look, mum, they've got rabbits in that pet shop.'

I didn't push it. I crossed my fingers and wished for my daughter's secrets always to be happy ones.

Grandad

Grandad, after my grandmother died, was rescued from loneliness and a fridge full of rotting bacon by my mother, the youngest of his three daughters. My earliest memory is of him sitting on the end of my bed while I, having covered the room in pink sick, anxiously waited for my parents to return from an evening out. He made no attempt to clean up the mess, or even to offer me words of reassurance, but I remember drawing some sense of comfort from the familiar figure regarding me silently, the ever present Woodbine dangling from his lower lip. Grandad always dressed formally in narrow grey suits which camouflaged the ash that fell constantly from his cigarettes. It was to my mother's chagrin that he never appeared to appreciate the function of ash trays. The cigarettes were such an integral part of him that he seemed reluctant to part with their residue.

His room, in contrast to the bright white modernity of the rest of the house, was a dark and musty cavern of antique furniture and dusty old Readers' Digest books. Grandad had been a travelling salesman for most of his life, selling leathergoods, and had retained a set of model seals (made out of real sealskin, my mother informed me disapprovingly) with which he allowed me to play with when I dared to enter his imposing quarters. This I did rarely, and always under the guise of an errand, taking him in the newspaper or a cup of tea, and I was rewarded with the seals and a hard boiled sweet, an infinite supply of which Grandad could produce from his grey trousers pocket. My mother did not approve of this for she blamed her own bad teeth on Grandad's generosity with confectionery. It was always with trepidation that I entered his room, and always with relief that I scurried out, sucking my sweet, into the light.

Grandad was a man of few words but his impeccable manners were noted by the local ladies to whom he always raised his hat in the street. He was a member of the local bowls' club which he attended almost every afternoon, occasionally to sit in the sun by the green, but more frequently to play whist with the other old men in the dark interior of the clubhouse. His great love was boxing and, in the event of a big fight, he would be invited into our living room to watch the television. There he would sit tense, gripping the arms of the chair and uttering aggressive little grunts and snorts, seemingly lost in the bloody world before him. I was enthralled by the transformation of this usually quiet and passive man and I would always look forward to the boxing match, not with any interest in the sport, but merely to watch Grandad watching. My mother was contemptuous of the old man's excitement and would leave me alone to stare in wonder at the grunting, air-punching creature which emerged from my grandfather's suit. It was on these occasions that, at my bedtime, I was obliged by Grandad's presence to kiss him goodnight, and I dreaded this more than any other encounter. As I approached, nervously smelling the tobacco and hair oil, he would extend his arms to my shoulders and grip me with his bony fingers, turning a saggy cheek towards my lips. Kissing the yellow cheek very briefly I was never quite quick enough to avoid the loose skin being partially sucked into my mouth, filling me with disgust. It was a revulsion that only the very young can feel for the very old and it left me full of an inexplicable terror.

It was hard to say when Grandad first began to change. At first I was told that his memory lapses were merely the inevitable forgetfulness associated with old age. He found it increasingly difficult to remember my name, calling me by the names of my aunts and, sometimes, by names I had never heard. My mother was frequently summoned to his room to locate objects he had misplaced, and he went less often to his club, sitting for hours in his armchair and calling for cups of tea which he invariably left to go cold by his side. One day, on one of his rare ventures into the outside world, Grandad did not return for his evening meal. My mother, covering her anxiety with irritation, left the dinner to burn and went to the bowls' club where, she was told, Grandad had left some hours previously. He was brought home just before dark by two policemen who had found him wandering through the gardens of the street where he had lived in his youth. Grandad refused to discuss the matter, and my mother managed to dissuade him from ever going back to his club. She employed the suggestion that 'tomorrow' would be a better day to visit and, on the following day, Grandad had always conveniently forgotten her words.

As Grandad's memory deteriorated his conversation became littered with repetitive questions and bizarre references to incidents from the past. Finally my mother could no longer tolerate the strain of the dinner-table and took to providing his meals on a tray in his room. It was often my job to retrieve the picked-over plates, and now I entered his domain with more confidence. As he regarded me with his blank gaze I felt secure in the knowledge that I was as unrecognisable as a stranger to him. Sleeping through the afternoons in his chair, Grandad would often pace the house in the middle of the night, waking my mother to ask her where the whist drive was. One night I was woken by the sound of my bedroom door opening and Grandad switched on the light, standing silently in striped pyjamas and staring with open confusion at the strange child before him. Disorientated and helpless he raised his palms as if seeking salvation and I, feeling bold, left my bed and led the old man by the hand back to his room. It was my father's idea to put a lock on the outside of Grandad's door and so the nocturnal wanderings ceased, although often I could hear the muffled knocking of a fist on wood.

As a child will learn basic tasks to increase its independence so Grandad, regressively, forgot all the skills of self-care and reclaimed the lessons he had long ago taught his daughter. Unable even to dress himself he once, to my extreme embarrassment, opened the front door to a group of my schoolfriends with his underpants over his head, his arms restricted and poking through the legs, and his wrinkled member pathetically displayed to the laughing children. He was, at this time, doubly incontinent and wore bulky pads which were referred to as 'Grandad's nappies' and which he always removed during the night and furiously threw around the room. Every morning I awoke to the sound of the washing machine's rhythmical hum and the humiliated cries of my grandfather being washed. One morning as I was eating breakfast the shouts became louder than usual and I caught the word 'bitch' escaping from behind the closed door, followed by the sound of a slap. My mother emerged, biting her lip, and hurried past me into the kitchen where I found her, leaning with her full weight against the sink and staring out of the window at the rose garden. I approached her from behind and tentatively put my arms around her waist, feeling the shudders of her body as she tried to suppress the tears and protect me from the burden which she was so adamant should not be mine.

It was then that I decided to kill Grandad. Rationalising any moral dilemma with the supposition that the old man was probably more miserable than he was making my mother, I plotted with a naïve confidence inspired by films and the great many adult books I had precociously read. My knowledge of murder incorporated stabbing, strangling, drowning, asphyxiation by a plastic bag, smashing the skull with a heavy object, shooting and poisoning. All except the latter two involved physically overpowering the victim and so these options were ruled out by virtue of my small stature. It was unlikely, at ten years old, that I could acquire a gun, and so I settled for poisoning. Rifling through the bathroom medicine cabinet I had already decided that the substance needed must be readily dissolved as it was to be placed inside the teapot of my grandfather's afternoon tray. The choice was limited but I discovered, with mounting excitement, an unopened packet of thirty soluble aspirin. Carefully I removed two, in case my mother had one of her headaches, and hid the rest in the pocket of my trousers. I slipped unnoticed from the bathroom to my bedroom where I hastily closed the door and sank down on the floor against it, my heart thumping. I removed the packet and read the instruction leaflet twice until satisfied that the contents would, indeed, do the trick. I noted with pleasure the final advice: 'Keep out of reach of children'.

I crept furtively downstairs and tried to walk nonchalantly into the kitchen. My mother was at the sink, scrubbing potatoes, and I was pleased to see that the tea tray was already laid out.
'Shall I take Grandad's tea in?' I asked casually.
'Oh would you?' replied my mother, 'I'll just put the kettle on.'
She filled the kettle, switched it on and then, to my relief, left the potatoes and went into the garden to bring in the washing. Quick as a flash I leapt to the tray, keeping one eye on my mother at the washing line and, with my hands hidden under the kitchen counter, I

removed the twenty-eight tablets from their foil cases and popped them into the teapot. My mission nearly complete, I raced back upstairs to my bedroom, stuffing the empty packaging under my bed to be disposed of later, and returned to my position on the kitchen stool, the blood pounding in my temples. My mother returned just as the kettle was boiling and I held my breath as she poured water into the teapot and replaced its lid.

'Leave it to brew for a minute,' she said.

I watched, in horror, as a white froth began to seep out from the edges of the teapot lid. Bubbling like a witches' cauldron my effervescent concoction poured furiously from the teapot, pushing the metal lid with its force and causing it to rattle up and down. My mother turned round. I had a sudden vision of the court, of the remand home, of never seeing my family again.

'What on earth . . . ?' she said. 'I can't have washed the teapot very well,' and with no more than a puzzled frown she emptied the contents down the sink, swilled the pot thoroughly and replaced it on the tray.

'Now,' she said, 'let's start again.'

Grandad lived for another three years, totally dependent on my mother but apparently unaware of who she was. On the one occasion that we attempted a holiday and placed Grandad temporarily in an old peoples' home he raised his feeble fist to my father and returned so distressed that my mother vowed never to leave him again. The matron of the home politely informed my parents that they would not be willing to have him back. When he died, silently, in his sleep, I awoke and lay in my bed waiting for morning and my mother to come in and tell me. I cried, briefly, but my surprise at the tears stopped them before my mother had left the room. I was instructed to wait in my bedroom while the doctor and the undertaker came, and when I finally went downstairs, Grandad had gone. There was just a strange smell left, different and more awful even than the stench of his soiled underwear, but by the evening it had disappeared.

Soon the old furniture disappeared too, and the books, and the furry seals, but the repainted room still retained a dark atmosphere which made the back of my neck prickle. Many years later, in that room which was now reserved for guests, while helping my mother to make the bed I saw her glance round the white walls and shiver.

'Poor old thing,' she said, plumping up the pillows, 'stuck in here for so many years. I still feel guilty about him.'

'You did all you could,' I replied. 'More than most would.'

My mother folded down the top sheet and looked intently at me.

'Still,' she said, 'we could have been nicer to him.'

Vincent and the Tooth Fairy

Vincent's front tooth was very, very loose. He could jiggle it backwards and forwards with his tongue and he could twist it from side to side with his fingers. All morning during lessons he jiggled it and twisted it, and at lunchtime he showed it to the girls and made them scream. Then at half past three, just as the bell rang for home-time, Vincent's tooth fell out.

'Put it under your pillow tonight,' said Vincent's Mum when he showed her. 'You have to leave it out for the Tooth Fairy.'

So that night Vincent climbed into bed and carefully placed his tooth under the pillow.

'Don't close the door,' he told his mum as she kissed him goodnight. 'I want to watch the Tooth Fairy fly in.'

'Oh you won't see her,' replied Vincent's mum. 'She's invisible.'

But Vincent knew the Tooth Fairy wasn't invisible. He knew she was a lovely lady with a silver dress and sparkly wings, and he was determined to stay awake to see her. But try as he might Vincent just could not keep his eyes open, and soon he was fast asleep.

Much, much later, when all the lights in the house were out and it was very dark, Vincent woke with a jump. He was sure he had heard a voice. He listened hard.

'Oi!'

There it was again. Vincent sat up in bed, switched on his bedside light and looked around, but no-one was there. He lay down again but as soon as his head touched the pillow he heard the voice.

'Oi! You!'

Vincent sat up again.

'That's better! Now just keep your head off that pillow for a minute while I get this tooth out.'

Vincent gently lifted the corner of the pillow and there, underneath, was a tiny little man about the size of his thumb. He was wearing brown overalls and a brown flat cap, and his little arms were wrapped around Vincent's tooth. Vincent stared in amazement as the tiny figure heaved and grunted under the weight of his burden.

'Who are you?' asked Vincent.

The little man stopped struggling and eyed him warily.

'I'm the Tooth Fairy of course,' he replied. 'Who did you think I was - Father Christmas?'

'B-but,' stammered Vincent, 'you don't look like a Tooth Fairy. I thought she was a lovely lady with a silver dress and sparkly wings.'

The little man sneered.

'Huh! You've obviously been reading too many books,' he said. 'Now, if you'd just be so kind and give me a hand with this whoppa - that's it - just put it on my back - that's the way!'

The little man, was almost bent double under the weight of the tooth, gave a big grunt and started walking off down the bed.

'Well thanks very much for the gnasher, Vince. See you again, mate!'

'Erm - hang on a minute,' Vincent said. 'Erm - what about the money?'

The little man stopped and looked round.

'Money?' he said.

'Yes,' said Vincent. 'I thought that's what the Tooth Fairy did - took the tooth and left money under the pillow.'

The man sighed.

'Not another one!' he groaned. 'As if my job isn't difficult enough as it is - now he's asking for money!'

Vincent felt embarrassed.

'I'm sorry,' he told the man. 'It's just - I thought - '

'I know, I know.' The man let the tooth slide down his back onto the bed and took off his flat cap. He scratched his little bald head.

'Look mate,' he said. 'I know you were expecting payment, but quite honestly it's bad enough lugging these great chompers around without having to carry a great big coin here as well.'

'You see,' continued the little man, 'it wasn't so bad in the old days - those silver sixpences were pretty small, but you can imagine a whopping big 10p piece on my back, or even a 50p piece! Not an easy job, I can tell you!'

'Oh I see,' said Vincent.

Seeing the disappointment on Vincent's face the man smiled.

'Aw, don't worry mate - I'll see what I can do when I get back.'

'Back?' said Vincent. 'Back where?'

The little man raised his eyes to the ceiling.

'Are you daft or what? *Fairyland*, of course! Where do you think I'm going - Bognor Regis?'

'Fairyland!' Vincent's eyes grew bigger and bigger. 'Is there really a Fairyland?'

'Well if there isn't,' said the little man patiently, 'just where do you suppose all the fairies live?'

'Oh, Wowee!' shouted Vincent pushing the bedclothes off. 'Oh take me back with you - please - I've always wanted to go to Fairyland.'

The little man shook his head slowly.

'Oh no, mate,' he said 'Sorry, but that's out of the question. No boys allowed in Fairyland you see.'

'Oh please,' said Vincent.

'No way,' said the little man, frowning. 'More than my job's worth.'

Suddenly Vincent had an idea.

'But listen,' he told the man. 'If I come back with you I can collect the coin and save you the trouble of bringing it all the way back.'

A gleam flickered in the little man's eyes.

'Well . . . I suppose you could just come and have a peep.'

'Oh great!' cried Vincent. 'How do we get there?'

'Easy,' the man told him. 'You just have to say the right words.'

And then he told Vincent some very special words to say.

There was a great rush of warm wind and Vincent felt himself falling down a long dark tunnel. He was falling so fast he could hardly breathe and he shut his eyes tight, hoping it wouldn't hurt when he landed at the bottom. As it was he never felt a thing. One minute he was falling and the next minute, when he opened his eyes, he was sitting in a huge, white marble room, at an enormous table with a silver cup in front of him.

'Chocolate milkshake?' said a voice.

Vincent looked up to see the most beautiful lady he could ever imagine. She had long silver hair which was as bright as fireworks, and she was wearing a silver dress studded with thousands of diamonds. And behind her shoulders Vincent could see the fluttering of her sparkly wings.

'I said do you want some chocolate milkshake?'

'Oh - oh yes please,' said Vincent, and the beautiful lady poured a glistening mixture into his silver cup.

'Now, Vincent,' she said as he took a gulp of the delicious drink. 'Stan tells me you want some money.'

'Stan?' Vincent was confused.

'Yes. Stan,' said the lady impatiently. 'Stan is the Tooth Removal Man - the fellow you presumably found under your pillow.'

'But he told me he was the Tooth Fairy,' said Vincent.

The lady sighed.

'Yes, well he would say that wouldn't he? I mean you wouldn't go giving away your teeth to any Tom, Dick or Harry would you?'

Vincent shook his head.

'You mean - he lied?'

The beautiful lady raised her eyebrows.

'Oh no, dear, not exactly, well maybe a little fib. But you see he was working *for* the Tooth Fairy, so it's all above board.'

Vincent's head began to spin.

'So where *is* the Tooth Fairy? He asked.

'Why right here of course,' said the beautiful lady. 'Who do you think I am - the Easter Bunny?'

Vincent looked at the beautiful Tooth Fairy and then glanced down to see Stan pulling at his pyjama leg.

'Sorry about that little misunderstanding,' said Stan. 'You see the Tooth Fairy doesn't have time to collect teeth anymore. She has to stay here to supervise the building of the castle.'

'Oh I see,' said Vincent, slurping his milkshake.

'Tell you what, mate,' said Stan. 'Shall I show you around?'

'What a splendid idea!' said the Tooth Fairy. 'Yes, Stan, take Vincent all around my castle and then bring him back for a chat. Perhaps then we can come to some arrangement.'

'You mean about my tooth?' said Vincent eagerly.

'Exactly,' said the Tooth Fairy.

So Vincent followed Stan around the enormous white marble castle, through rooms as big as palaces and up towers as high as skyscrapers. Although it seemed to take hours and hours to walk all the way round, Vincent didn't feel tired, and he was sorry when finally Stan said it was nearly time to go home.

'Just one last room,' said Stan. 'The newest wing - the Tooth Fairy is always building new rooms you see.'

Through a tall marble archway Vincent could see thousands of little people moving slabs of marble with tiny cranes the size of Vincent's hand. The new room was bigger than the biggest building Vincent had ever seen, and the rows of white marble slabs twinkled in the sunshine like a smile. Vincent thought about it. Like a smile! He looked again at the rows of marble slabs, the white marble walls, and the high marble towers.

'Hey, Stan!' he shouted. 'That's not marble at all is it?'

Stan grinned.

'Well, Vince,' he said. 'What did you think we did with all the teeth?'

In astonishment Vincent followed Stan back to where the Tooth Fairy was waiting with a fresh jug of chocolate milkshake.

'So, Vincent,' she said. 'Would you like the rest of your teeth to complete the most beautiful castle in Fairyland?'

'Oh yes!' cried Vincent. 'Of course I would - and you can have every one of my teeth for free. I don't want any money for them, truly.'

'How kind of you,' replied the Tooth Fairy. 'But of course we must pay you - and your generosity will be rewarded well.'

And with that the beautiful Tooth Fairy plucked one of the tiny diamonds off her dress and handed it to Vincent.

'Will that do my dear?' she smiled.

Vincent stared at the sparkling diamond in delight.

'Oh, Wowee, thanks!' he said. 'And thank you for letting me see the castle - could I come again do you think?'

'Of course,' said the Tooth Fairy. 'Anytime you want to come just say the special words that Stan taught you, and you'll be here. Now do you remember them?'

Vincent thought and thought but he could not remember one of those words.

'Well,' said the Tooth Fairy. 'You'll be needing them to get home so listen carefully . . . '

And then the Tooth Fairy repeated those special words.

When Vincent woke up he was in his own bed and the first thing he did was try to remember those special words. But of course he could not remember a single one. The next thing he did was put his hand under his pillow, and his fingers closed around something cold and hard. There, glittering on his palm, was a perfect diamond. Vincent gasped with delight but no sooner had he looked at the beautiful jewel than it seemed to disappear before his eyes. Vincent blinked, looked again, and there on his palm was a brand new pound coin!

Vincent sighed. It was nice to have a whole pound, of course, but he would like to have kept the diamond to remind him of Fairyland. Since he had forgotten the special words he didn't know how to get back there. Wait a minute though! Vincent suddenly remembered what the Tooth Fairy had said. She wanted the rest of his teeth to complete her castle! Vincent put his finger into the gap in his mouth and almost shouted for joy. Another tooth was starting to wobble! And so, jiggling and twisting his wobbly tooth, Vincent went to tell his Mum all about his adventure.

Jimmy's Story

Jimmy used to take out his eye and show it to you. On the palm of his hand it did not look like an eye at all, more like a marble. One day, as he showed his treasure to a group of squealing children in the car park, Fat Gary whacked Jimmy's arm from underneath so that the eye shot into the air and winked in the sunlight before rolling under the line of parked Cortinas. It took an hour to retrieve it, and the small council estate came to life as neighbours gathered on the balconies to watch Jimmy scrambling frantically between the cars, all but his short legs disappearing beneath them.

''Ere - over 'ere, Jim - I think I can see it.'

Finally he emerged, triumphant, holding up the glass eye like a trophy to the applauding crowds, before sucking it clean and replacing it in its socket.

He was a small, middle-aged man with a large beaked nose and a chirpy smile. Everyone knew Jimmy. He popped up everywhere like a sparrow, his beady eye fixed on the East End hubbub of disputes and dramas. He had encyclopaedic knowledge of the minutiae of everyday Cockney life, and could give you a current update on anybody's activities, domestic situation, or state of health.

'I don't want to get involved,' he would say, 'but I'll tell you something . . . '

The kids loved Jimmy. On most evenings he could be seen crouching for hours in the car park, mending bicycles with a group of dirty children fighting for his attentions. Often, returning from his ten-hour shift at the warehouse and just gasping for a cup of tea and a read of the paper, Jimmy would be greeted at his front door by a snotty tear-stained face. He always had a sympathetic ear, a bit of advice, or some practical tip for a broken toy. That was how Jimmy lost half his vision, when Fat Gary gave him the suction gun to mend. The toy had been jammed with a pencil and Jimmy, peering down the barrel to release the obstruction, shot himself in the eye. He never blamed Fat Gary, though. Jimmy never blamed the kids for anything. He loved kids, and it almost broke his heart to read stories in 'The

Mirror' about cruelty to children. Once he had read a story about a little girl who had been locked in a cupboard for a year. There was a photo of her, a tiny emaciated figure with enormous eyes in a ghostly face, and little sharp protruding teeth bared in the grimace of a skull. Jimmy nearly cried when he saw that photo. He couldn't even finish reading the story.

Jimmy lived with his father and his brother, Reggie. The first floor council flat was divided into three quite separate bachelor bedsits, and the three men met only in the kitchen where they prepared their separate meals. There was a television in each bedroom, and one in the kitchen, so you didn't miss anything when you were making tea. Dad was a large man who always wore a yachting cap. His emphysema kept him confined to the flat, from where he developed startlingly simplistic theories about the problems of the world. His theories were rarely disputed, as Jimmy was generally out at work, and Reggie was not given to philosophical debate.

Reggie was also large in build, but with an endearingly childish smile and a vacant gaze. His head was rather too big for his body, giving the impression that he might topple over at any moment. Every morning, as he stumbled off to the day centre clutching his ex-army lunch-box, the kids would shout after him,
'All right, Reggie?'
'Off to school, Reggie?' and he would turn, slowly, sometimes with a wave of his big hand, and occasionally with an incoherent greeting. Reggie had difficulty with conversation and his voice seemed trapped somewhere in his throat. When addressed directly he would cough, growl and, with a huge effort, finally force out the words with a fiercesome bellow. But Reggie wasn't fierce. In fact, apart from the time Fat Gary had tried to grab his lunch box, no-one had ever seen Reggie angry. Jimmy had always looked after his brother. He was sharp, and from an early age he had learned to be sharp enough for two. He had never really minded that Reggie wasn't normal. But, then again, Jimmy wasn't really normal either.

Jimmy always knew he was different to the other boys. He liked girls, certainly, but he always knew that there was a difference between liking something and wanting to touch it. Jimmy never wanted to touch a girl. In fact, the thought of it made him feel sick. The girls liked Jimmy because he was kind; he listened to their troubles and he looked at their new clothes. But they did not seem to want to touch him either. So it all worked out quite well for Jimmy. He often thought to himself that things could be a lot worse.

Jimmy had plenty of friends, he had the occasional weekend in Amsterdam, and he had Gordon. Gordon and Jimmy had known each other for fifteen years and Gordon was fond of saying that they were like an old married couple. Jimmy didn't feel married to Gordon, though, perhaps because he only saw him once a week. Gordon lived with his invalid mother in Essex, but every Saturday afternoon he got a friend to look after Mother, hopped on the train, and spent a sweaty three hours locked in Jimmy's bedroom. He was a pale, bald man, who looked very much like a bank clerk, which is what he had been before he gave up his career to nurse Mother. Jimmy did not think he was in love with Gordon, but the arrangement suited him. Love, like a fast car, or winning the pools, was one of those things that happened to other people and eluded Jimmy. Besides, he was fond of Gordon. Sometimes, however, when Gordon had left, Jimmy would sit on the crumpled bed and watch the sun go down over the gas works, and he would get a funny feeling inside which stopped him turning on the TV or picking up the paper. He could not exactly describe that feeling, but it was scary, and Jimmy knew that he had to watch the sun disappear before the feeling would go away.

It was raining the last Saturday that Gordon visited Jimmy. Fat Gary banged on the front door just as he was leaving and, after stinging him for fifty pence, turned his attentions to Jimmy.
''Ere, let us in for tea, Jim.'
Jimmy was tired and looking forward to a quiet smoke and a read of the racing page. Behind Fat Gary stood a tall Bengali boy whom he did not recognise. Both boys were dripping wet and shivering.
'Come on, Jimmy, let us in - Mam's chucked us out again.' Fat Gary pursed his lips and opened his slitty eyes as wide as they would go in an attempt, it seemed, to appear like an abandoned puppy.
'This is Tariq,' he nodded behind him. 'He's got nowhere to go

neither.'

The Bengali boy smiled shyly at Jimmy, flashing a set of perfect white teeth, and shifting uncomfortably from one foot to the other.

'Please, Jim.'

Jimmy sighed.

'All right, just a quick cuppa,' he said, and Fat Gary led the way to his bedroom while Jimmy went to the kitchen to put the kettle on. He switched on the TV and was pleased to see the end of the last race.

'Phwoar,' shouted Fat Gary from the bedroom. 'Smells like a Sumo-wrestler's jockstrap in 'ere.'

Jimmy smiled and began preparing the tea. A tray was always laid out in the kitchen with a teapot, cups, sugar bowl, and a mug full of water with teaspoons in it. Jimmy opened a cupboard, took out a packet of custard creams, and was putting them on a plate when Dad wheezed into the kitchen.

'Tea's up,' said Jimmy.

'Ah, just the thing,' replied Dad. 'Gordon gone?'

Dad had become accustomed to Gordon's visits and, without exactly giving his approval, had managed to convey a certain amicability towards him. Dad maintained a silence regarding Jimmy's difference, ever since his initial outburst of outrage, many years before, which had started and ended with the words 'No son of mine'. After this tirade, which had left Jimmy shaking for a week, it was never mentioned again, except just once. That was when Dad had picked up a photo which had dropped out of Jimmy's pocket. It was of Jimmy, in Amsterdam, dressed from head to toe in black rubber, and wearing a rubber mask with a ventilator tube.

'What's this?' Dad had asked, turning the photo sideways, and then upside down.

Jimmy had taken a big breath and said, 'It's me.'

Dad had frowned, squinted hard at the picture, and then looked straight at Jimmy. He looked confused.

'Sometimes I wonder what I did wrong,' he said.

Jimmy carefully carried three cups of tea and the custard creams into his bedroom. Fat Gary was lying outstretched on the bed, watching TV. Tariq was standing looking at the 'Gay Men's Calendar' on Jimmy's wall. Mr September was a blonde Adonis wearing a small fig-leaf and a foolish smile.

'Here you are then, lads. D'you take sugar, Tariq? I put two in anyway - I don't know anyone who doesn't take two sugars!'

The boy turned and smiled at Jimmy.

'You like men?' he asked, taking the tea.

Fat Gary snorted and sat up.

''Course he does, he's a fucking woofter. That's his boyfriend just left - ain't that right Jimmy?'

Jimmy ignored him and turned to Tariq.

'That's the way I am,' he said simply.

Tariq smiled again. He sipped the tea delicately and then placed the cup on the window sill. His long fingers were smooth and brown and he pointed one straight at Jimmy and then at the calendar.

'It is not wrong,' he said.

Fat Gary chortled and flopped back down on the bed.

'Just be careful, Tariq,' he sniggered. 'Don't bend over in here without looking behind you,' and he convulsed with laughter, his large belly wobbling between the gap in his shirt and jeans. Jimmy shook his head at Fat Gary and then turned to the Bengali boy. Tariq was watching him intently with his large brown eyes.

It was still light when Jimmy finished work on Monday, so he thought he would take a stroll round the community garden and look at the last of his roses. Fat Gary and Tariq were leaning against the shed, smoking and watching a group of younger children throwing stones at a cat, and Jimmy felt a stab of pleasure at seeing the handsome Bengali boy again. It was a warm evening and Tariq was wearing a white short-sleeved T-shirt which revealed his lean arms, innocently smooth but with well-defined muscles. His skin glowed golden in the last rays of the sun.

'Oi, Jimmy,' yelled Fat Gary. 'Lend us a quid.'

'No chance,' said Jimmy, 'I'm broke till Friday.'

'Lend us a fiver Friday then?' shouted Gary.

Jimmy chuckled and began examining the roses. There were still a few fine blooms, and he rather hoped Tariq would come over and admire his labours. Carefully he pulled towards him a large white rose, delicately tinged with pink, and bent to sniff it, letting out a noisily enthusiastic sigh of appreciation. Sure enough the two teenagers sauntered over.

'Whassat then?' asked Fat Gary.

'Madame Alfred Carriere,' replied Jimmy, proudly. 'Smell it.'

'Who the fuck's she then - some French bird?' asked Fat Gary, grabbing the rose with his sausage fingers and sniffing loudly.

'Can't smell nothing,' he said.

'Watch it, Gary,' Jimmy warned. 'Oh Gawd - look what you've done!'

The bloom hung limply on its broken stem.

'Madame Alfred fucking Carriere,' sneered Fat Gary, unperturbed. 'Fucking poncey name - they should've called it after me, Gary Smith.'

He laughed loudly.

'Eh Tariq? The Gazza rose!'

Jimmy tutted and with a reluctant frown plucked the rose from its stem and regarded it mournfully.

'Gawd, you're an animal, Gary,' he said. 'Shouldn't be allowed near anything pretty.'

He smelt the rose again and then, on impulse, handed it to Tariq.

'Here,' he said. 'You have it.' Then he blushed and added hastily, 'Give it to your girlfriend.'

But it was too late. Fat Gary's eyes leered and his face opened into a broad grin of greenish teeth.

'Aah, look!' he cried gleefully. 'Aah, ain't that sweet? He's given 'im a flower - hey kids, over'ere, look at this.'

The group of children immediately left the cat and came rushing over.

'Aw Jimmy - can I have one Jimmy?'

' Jimmy, give me one too.'

They gathered round, grubby hands outstretched.

'Please Jimmy, can I have a flower?'

'Oh Gawd,' cried Jimmy. 'Now look what I've started!'

Patiently he explained to the children the unique and unrepeatable circumstances surrounding the plucking of Madame Alfred Carriere, until the youngest child, six year old David Stassinopolous, jumped onto Jimmy's back and began their usual boisterous manoeuvres.

'Me next, me next!' shouted the other children, and each in turn was lifted, swung, thrown and turned upside down, screaming with delight. Tariq stood silently, awkwardly holding the rose, while Fat

Gary took over the task of stoning the cat. Eventually Jimmy, red-faced, was overtaken by a fit of coughing, and tried unsuccessfully to prise the arms of David Stassinopolous from around his neck.

'Right that's enough,' he gasped. 'Come on now, get off.'

'Aw Jimmy,' wailed David, wrapping his legs tightly around Jimmy's waist and wiping his nose on his shoulder. 'Just once more.'

'Now, come on,' said Jimmy. 'It's time for my tea,' and the small boy slipped grudgingly to the floor.

'Coming out tomorrow, Jimmy?' chorused the children, as he started walking off towards his flat.

'Maybe,' Jimmy smiled over his shoulder at the kids and was surprised to see Tariq coming after him. The boy smiled as he caught up with Jimmy and began walking in step with him. The rose, Jimmy noticed, had disappeared.

'All right, Tariq?'

The boy seemed nervous, apprehensive.

'Jimmy, I - ,' he faltered, and then blurted out, 'Have you really no money?'

Jimmy laughed.

'Not a lot,' he replied. 'Why do you ask?'

'I need ten pounds,' said Tariq. 'To borrow.'

It was a day's wages, and Jimmy knew better than to lend the kids money, but something in the boy's face made him bite back his instinctive refusal. There was a desperate urgency in his eyes, and although Jimmy had seen his share of desperation, he was touched.

'Only till the weekend,' said Tariq. 'I beg you.'

Jimmy thought of his savings: forty quid in a jam jar for his next trip to Amsterdam.

'All right. Just this once,' he said. 'It's in the flat.'

Jimmy made a pot of tea while Tariq went into the bedroom. When he took the tea in the boy was again standing staring at the calendar.

'He is handsome.' said Tariq.

Jimmy was taken aback by the sincerity of the statement, without the usual smirk of a taunt.

'Certainly is,' Jimmy replied. 'But out of my league, I'm afraid.'

'You like looking at him?' asked Tariq persistently.

Jimmy chuckled.

'Nosey bugger, ain't you?' but the boy's artless curiosity mellowed him.

'Look, I'll tell you something, Tariq,' he said. 'There's never been any harm in looking. There's a lot of things in this world to look at - some of 'em you can touch, and some of 'em you can't. As long as you know which is which, you don't do nobody no harm.'

The boy stared at him for a moment, and then a smile slowly spread across his face.

'So who do you touch, Jimmy?'

Jimmy laughs.

'Now that would be telling,' he said. 'Here. I'll get you that tenner.'

Tuesday was wet again and Jimmy's bedroom was full of children watching TV. Jimmy was in the kitchen preparing the evening meal when he heard a knock at the door. It was Tariq, barely recognisable in a hooded jacket, and holding out a small metal object.

'For you, Jimmy,' he said.

It was a steel penknife, made in the shape of a fish.

'For you,' repeated the boy, thrusting the knife towards Jimmy. Jimmy blinked, and his glass eye closed as it always did when he was overcome with emotion. He took the knife, opened the blade, and gently ran his finger along it.

'Aw, thanks Tariq,' he said. 'Coming in? I was just making me tea.'

Tariq followed him into the kitchen and perched on a stool while Jimmy removed a small meat pie from the oven. On the formica counter lay two buttered slices of Mother's Pride and Jimmy placed the pie on top of one slice, covering it liberally with H P sauce. Then, removing a fruit cake from its tupperware box, he cut a slice and placed it on top of the pie.

'There!' he said, grinning at Tariq. 'That should sweeten it up lovely,' and he placed the other slice of bread on top of the concoction and gave it two hearty thumps with his palm.

'Better eat it in here, otherwise the kids will all want some,' said Jimmy. 'You want a bit Tariq?'

The boy shook his head vigorously.

'No, no it's all right,' he said.

'Suit yourself,' said Jimmy, 'all the more for me,' and he opened his mouth as wide as it would go and attacked the sandwich, brown sauce spurting over his face and hands. At that moment there were squeals from the bedroom. Jimmy lowered the sandwich and cocked his head on one side, frowning. A man's deep voice said,

'Spread 'em.'

'Oh, blimey!' cried Jimmy, dropping his sandwich and running into the bedroom, closely followed by Tariq. Four children were huddled round the video recorder and Tariq just glimpsed a grainy picture of leather and naked skin before Jimmy switched off the set and turned to face the audience.

'Who put that on?' he demanded. His face was white except for the smear of brown sauce on his chin. The children looked at their hands.

'I've told you not to play with the video,' said Jimmy. 'Who put it on?'

David Stanissopolous hiccoughed. His sister, Charlene, giggled.

'Right! Home - all of you,' ordered Jimmy.

The children trooped out silently. Tariq and Jimmy listened to the bang of the front door, the sound of feet running down the stairs, and the laughter that exploded at ground level and faded into the distance. Jimmy shook his head.

'Those kids are well out of order,' he said.

Tariq said nothing.

'Well out of order,' repeated Jimmy, fetching his sandwich from the kitchen and switching on the news. 'Let's see what's new then.'

They sat side-by-side on the bed, their boots hanging over the edge of the pink nylon eiderdown.

Tariq sat silently through the news, Emmerdale Farm, and Coronation Street.

Occasionally he would reach for Jimmy's tobacco tin, nudge Jimmy's arm, and raise his eyebrows. Each time Jimmy said, 'Sure, help yourself, no need to ask,' and the boy rolled a cigarette with painstaking care. Jimmy watched the delicate way he licked the paper with his pink tongue. After examining the rolled cigarette closely, Tariq then leaned back against the wall behind the bed and reverently struck a match, pausing until the flame almost burned his finger before lighting up. He smoked with a series of short, deep sucks, blowing the smoke in a fast stream at the ceiling. Between cigarettes the boy stared at the television screen and responded to Jimmy's frequent exclamations and comments with a smile, but he showed no apparent interest in the programmes. Jimmy wondered if he was really watching them. It seemed as though he was waiting for something.

At nine o'clock Jimmy switched off the TV. He was tired and his shift began at six the next morning.
'I'm going to turn in soon,' he said. 'Fancy a cuppa before you go?'
Tariq seemed to emerge slowly from a dream. He squinted at Jimmy and then frowned and bit his lip.
'I need more money,' he said. 'Until Saturday.'
Jimmy sucked in his breath.
'Look I'm sorry, mate, but I can't help you there. I'm earning bugger all as it is, and half the stuff in here ain't paid for yet.'
Tariq looked at him.
'I really am sorry, mate, but I'm the wrong person to ask.'
The boy half-turned on the bed and faced Jimmy directly. He leaned forward slightly and lowered his voice.
'I'm in trouble, Jimmy.'
Jimmy could smell the boy's spicy breath. He was so close that he could feel the heat of his body.
'What kind of trouble?' asked Jimmy, but his own voice suddenly seemed a long way off and he knew that his question would remain unanswered. He heard nothing but the blood roaring in his ears as he saw Tariq's mouth open just slightly, and felt the boy's spidery fingers crawl lightly up his leg.

At six o'clock on Wednesday evening Jimmy's front door was kicked in. Jimmy arrived home from the warehouse at six-thirty to find Dad and Reggie sitting in the kitchen, drinking tea out of the two cups which had miraculously remained unbroken amidst the chaotic destruction. Dad looked calm, although his yachting cap was missing. Reggie was trembling so much that his tea slopped over the sides of his cup and splashed onto the floor. Smeared over the sink, in red letters, was the word 'Nonce'. Jimmy approached the dripping word, and put a finger into the letter 'N', and examined the substance closely.
'Ketchup,' said Dad. 'But it would've been your blood if you'd been here.'

'Who was it?' asked Jimmy. His face had drained of colour.

'Gary's dad, and the father of that little Greek kid. And another bloke I didn't recognise.'

Jimmy rolled a cigarette.

'They'll be back,' said Dad.

'I'm going to buy an ice-cream,' said Jimmy.

But already he could hear murmurs from outside the front door. He paused, checked the loose change in his pocket, and then opened the door. Under his balcony stood a group of neighbours, six or seven men and women, and although he knew them well, it took Jimmy a few seconds to recognise them. Their faces were somehow different.

'There 'e is.'

'Fucking nonce.'

'Would you believe it - a child molester living right on your doorstep!'

The last words came from a large sweating woman in a loose floral smock and slippers. Gary's mother, Brenda, was standing with her hands on her hips, looking at Jimmy and chewing gum. Jimmy thought of his ice-cream, but the group was baring teeth like a pack of dogs. He wondered if he should just walk straight past them, if they would let him, but he remained outside his flat and stretched out his hands before him on the balcony wall.

'Look, I've done nothing wrong,' he said. 'I don't know what the problem is, but I've done nothing to be ashamed of.'

Brenda sneered.

'Nothing to be ashamed of?' She pointed a finger straight at Jimmy. 'Luring innocent children into your bedroom! Showing 'em filth! Touching *my son*!' Her voice rose to a screech. 'Nothing to be ashamed of?'

Jimmy looked bewildered. His glass eye closed.

'I'm going to buy an ice-cream,' he said. 'You can't stop me. I'm a free man and I've done nothing wrong.'

But he stayed on the balcony, and did not move until the police car drew up outside the flat.

'Things could be worse,' said Jimmy to the prison psychologist, Kenneth Edwards. They sat at either side of a large wooden table with an ash tray in the middle. Jimmy looked forward to Kenneth's monthly visits as the young man had an unlimited supply of Marlborough and, at the end of each session, he always handed Jimmy five cigarettes.

'The education classes are doing me the world of good,' said Jimmy. 'I can just about write a decent letter these days. And art! I never thought I was any good at it, but you'd be surprised.' He smiled at Kenneth.

'Have you thought any more about what we were talking about last time?' asked the psychologist.

'What's that, then?'

'About the boy,' Kenneth said. 'About Tariq.'

'I've told you,' said Jimmy. 'I don't know what the kid's game is, but when I get out of here I'm going to wring his bloody neck.'

Kenneth sighed and lit another Marlborough.

'That kid's got a lot to answer for,' continued Jimmy. 'Saying I drugged him, tied him up, kept him prisoner! What a story! Why's he do that then? You're a psychologist - what makes a kid lie like that?'

Kenneth took a long pull on his cigarette and then looked at Jimmy over the top of his small gold-rimmed spectacles.

'Jimmy,' he said slowly. 'You've got to start accepting things.'

Jimmy wished Kenneth wouldn't stare at him like that. It reminded him of the teachers at school.

'I don't know what you want me to accept,' he said. 'Do you want me to accept that I've been banged up for four years because of a lying little thief?'

'Jimmy,' Kenneth said. 'Sometimes it's much easier to deny something than to face it. Guilt is not a pleasant emotion.'

'What?' Jimmy's forehead creased. 'You talk in bloody riddles you do.'

'I think you understand what I'm saying, Jimmy,' said Kenneth.

'Well I don't,' Jimmy replied firmly. 'I don't understand a bloody word of it. You tell me I've got to talk about what I'm feeling and when I tell you, all you do is say it's the wrong answer. Can I have another fag?'

'It's time to finish now, anyway,' said Kenneth. 'I hope you'll think about the things we've discussed. You're coming up for parole soon and it's important that you come to terms with things.'

Jimmy gave a little snort and waited. Kenneth opened his Marlborough packet and carefully removed five cigarettes. He pointed them at Jimmy, tapping them on the table to emphasise his words, before dropping them at arm's length.

'Think about what I've said, Jimmy. I'll see you in four weeks.'

When Jimmy had left, Kenneth Edwards sat for a long time at the table, pulling his beard. This was a difficult case, and he knew that if he did not make some headway soon, Jimmy would be serving his full seven year sentence. Kenneth could not help rather liking the odd little glass-eyed man with his indefatigable optimism. He had been pleasantly surprised by the reality of the 'monster' he had read so much about.

'Paedophile ring cracked', the tabloid headlines had screamed, and the local social service department basked in a new confidence, flaunting Jimmy as their spolia opima. It was interesting that in court all the children involved, under cross-examination, retracted their stories. Only the sixteen-year old Bengali boy's evidence was finally used to send Jimmy down.

It was Christmas Eve when Jimmy received the letter. He was watching television with Charles, the magician. There was no television room and the set was chained to the bare corridor wall outside the fourteen cells of the inmates who, for reasons of their own safety, were segregated from the main body of the prison. They were a strange bunch, Jimmy thought, but nice enough once you got used to their quirks. Charles, for instance, often used his conjuring expertise to acquire extra benefits from his neighbours. Charles did not call it stealing, of course. He referred to it as 'the magic of redistribution'. He was a thin, silver-haired man with an educated accent and abnormally long fingers, and he was inside for having sexual intercourse with a twelve-year old girl. Charles had no apparent shame about this fact, and often spent hours reminiscing to Jimmy about the illicit relationship.

'It was love, you see,' he would sigh. 'That's what nobody ever understood. Love knows no laws.'

Jimmy kept an open mind about Charles' past. Not knowing much about love, he felt unqualified to pass judgement.

'Oi, Nobby!' one of the warders called. 'Letter for you.'

Jimmy trotted up to the office. He was used to his new nickname, although he still didn't understand why everyone referred to him as such. He couldn't complain, however. He got on well with all the screws and, after an initial month of unpleasant remarks and the occasional kick in the shins, he had never had a moment's trouble.

'Here you are, Nobby.'

The warder held out the opened letter but seemed to be evading Jimmy's eye. The white envelope was type-written and Jimmy unfolded the thick watermarked paper in wonder. The printed heading read, 'James Caulfield & Sons. Solicitors,' and the letter was sent to inform him, regretfully, that Gordon was dead. Jimmy read the letter twice, put it in the pocket of the coarse, blue prison trousers, and went to lie down on his bed. He could not think of anything except Gordon's white face on the day of his last visit. He had lost a lot of weight but avoided Jimmy's questions about his health, saying it was his usual 'tummy troubles'. But Jimmy had known there was more to it than that. At the time he had wondered why Gordon looked so frightened.

Charles soon came into Jimmy's cell and, when he learned about Gordon, uncharacteristically produced his tobacco tin.

'What a dreadful thing, old boy,' he said kindly. 'What a perfectly bloody thing.'

Jimmy just felt numb.

'Have a good cry, old chap,' advised Charles. 'Good to get it out.'

But Jimmy didn't cry. He felt as though there was nothing left inside him, not even tears.

Kenneth Edwards sat looking at the report he had written, thinking that the neat type-face did justice to his insightful conclusions.

'I can't complain,' Jimmy was saying. 'The food's getting worse, but at least the heating's working again. You know, they gave us shepherd's pie last night and it was just about all carrot. I mean, they should at least have the decency to call it carrot pie. Why raise your hopes?'

He looked questioningly at the psychologist.

'Talking of raising hopes,' said Kenneth. 'Your application for parole is going before the board next week.'

'Well,' said Jimmy. 'There's a problem with that.'

Kenneth leant forward eagerly.

'Yes, Jimmy,' he said. 'There is a problem.'

'You see, Ken,' said Jimmy. 'It's Gordon. I was going to live with Gordon - he asked me to when his mother died - but now he's gone, there's nowhere for me to go. I can't go back to the estate. Dad and Reggie have been re-housed but there's no room for me there. I'm in a bit of a fix, you see.'

'Hmm,' said Kenneth. 'I am aware of that situation, Jimmy, but there are also other, more important problems.'

Jimmy looked surprised.

'Like what?'

Kenneth drew on his cigarette.

'Jimmy,' he said. 'You must understand that one of the first things the parole board will want to know is if the applicant has come to terms with his crime. If he has accepted it, worked through his feelings.'

Kenneth looked down the report.

'And shown remorse,' he added.

Jimmy clenched his teeth and counted to ten.

'How many times do I have to tell you,' he said finally. 'How many times do I have to tell you I'm innocent? I've got nothing to admit, to accept, to feel guilty about, however you put it. I've done nothing wrong.'

Kenneth pulled at his beard.

'Look,' said Jimmy. 'Let me put it another way. Imagine yourself in my situation.'

Kenneth raised an eyebrow.

'Well, imagine one of the screws runs in here now, all bleeding, and says 'Kenneth Edwards beat me up."

'I really don't think - '

'Just listen,' ordered Jimmy. 'Imagine everyone believes that screw, and everyone thinks you attacked him, although you never touched him. Imagine that.'

'Jimmy, this is really quite beside the point.'

'No it ain't - it's just the same.'

Jimmy banged his fist on the table. In his excitement his voice grew louder and little droplets of spittle flew out of his mouth.

'Now listen, Ken. Everyone says you beat up the screw so they lock you in a cell, give you filth to eat, half an ounce of stale tobacco a week, and make you shit in a bucket next to your bed.'

Kenneth shifted uncomfortably in his chair but remained silent.

'But suppose everyone realises you didn't do it. They all know, but they can't lose face and admit they locked up an innocent man, so they say to you, 'OK Edwards, if you say you beat up that screw and say you're sorry, you can go free.''

Jimmy leaned back in his chair and smiled proudly.

'Well? What would you do?'

'Really, Jimmy, there is no room here for hypothetical fantasies.'

'Answer me.'

Jimmy's voice was suddenly unavoidably commanding.

'Well,' said Kenneth nervously. 'I think, if that was the only way to freedom - I think -er -I would probably say I'd done it.'

Jimmy looked at the psychologist in astonishment.

'What? But you never did it!'

Kenneth shrugged. A patch of red crept above his beard.

'Sometimes we have to compromise, Jimmy.'

Jimmy continued to stare at him. Slowly his glass eye began to close.

'I will never, ever admit to something I'm not guilty of,' he said quietly.

'It's time to finish,' said Kenneth, shortly. 'I'll give my report to the board.'

Jimmy waited, but Kenneth made no move towards his cigarettes.

'I'm disappointed, Jimmy,' said Kenneth. 'I'll see you in four weeks.'

They both looked at the packet of Marlborough on the table.

'Goodbye Jimmy,' said Kenneth.

Jimmy returned to his cell and lay on the bed. He thought that perhaps, in an ideal world, he would have punched Kenneth Edwards in the face. That's how it would have happened on television, anyway. Jimmy sighed a long sigh and screwed up his face very tight. He had planned for his parole. The first thing he was going to do was go to Al's café and order sausage, chips, double egg and baked beans. The second thing was to go down 'The Bear', see Georgie and all the rest, and have a large rum and black. Keeping his eyes firmly shut, Jimmy tried to imagine the faded red velvet chairs in 'The Bear'. Just for a moment he felt a stab of panic as he wondered if he would ever see them again. That's another thing that Gordon had said, that time was running out.

'Oi, Nobby! Letter for you.'

The envelope came hurtling through the door, and, although Jimmy raised his head to see it land, it was a long time before he wearily rolled off the bed and picked it up. It was Dad's familiar handwriting and Jimmy bit his lip as he sat back down on the bed. He studied the name and address closely, postponing both the pleasure and the pain of the contents. And then, suddenly, he laughed delightedly.

'Well, look at that!' he exclaimed, his face radiant with glee.

The postage stamp had not been franked and Jimmy, chuckling to himself, began to carefully peel it from the envelope.

Three Minute Warning

Above ground there was an icy November wind. It was five o'clock when I joined the rush and slipped into the moving line heading underground. My legs became a section of the giant millipede as we marched with faceless purpose past the busker singing 'Lay, Lady, Lay'. We marched past a young man slumped against the wall, his shaved head nearly touching the ground. Brown vomit pumped out of him, making a little foaming stream alongside the commuters.

The wintry air vanished and was replaced by hot gusts of bad breath from the tunnel. As we reached the platform the line of people dispersed and spread, now separate beings searching for a place to stand and wait. I found my space, so close to the next that I could feel the suck and blow of neighbouring lungs. The indicator said 'Edgware. 3 minutes.'

Next to me, attracting furtive glances, stood a tall black girl dressed in skin-tight P V C. She looked like a mannequin amongst the grey suits and overcoats. Her waist-length hair was straightened to a shimmering cloak which partly hid the iridescence of her skin and the shiny black plastic contours of her body. She was so thin you could have joined your hands around her waist. There seemed to be no room there for her internal organs.

The air was hazy and I remembered Daniel telling me that the haze was clouds of skin flake.
'Thousands of particles of dying people,' he said. 'The body sheds skin all the time and it collects in the tunnels. It can't escape.'
I tried not to breath.
The indicator said 'Edgware. 2 minutes.'

The people had opened their newspapers and their books, above which many pairs of eyes intermittently rose in the direction of the black girl. She was biting her full red lower lip and her huge eyes flashed up and down the platform. She shifted her position, moving her weight from one leg to the other. The graceful angles of her long bones seemed awkwardly imprisoned and her head jerked this way and that.

'You don't know who you're breathing in,' Daniel had said. 'Every breath down there is a lungful of someone else's cells.'

Beads of perspiration began to appear on the girl's forehead. She moved her large P V C bag from one shoulder to the other. The man in front of me, standing on the edge of the platform, turned and stared straight at her. The indicator said 'Edgware. 1 minute.'

He was an ordinary looking man, neither handsome nor ugly, young nor old. He was wearing a grey overcoat. He could have been anyone's father, brother, husband. He turned and looked at the black girl directly, without the cover of a newspaper, and he kept his eyes upon her until he had seen enough. He looked from the very top of head right down to her high-heeled patent leather boots. And then he looked at me.

I knew, when he looked at me, that he was going to jump. He stared right into my eyes and I knew, before all those others who were reading their papers, stealing glances at the black girl, and watching the indicator which said 'train approaching'. I think I opened my mouth.

It was not so much a jump as a slide. It was as though the life left his body at the moment he stepped forward. He looked like a puppet when you let go of the strings, and he crumpled onto the tracks with perfect timing. My eyes instinctively closed but I heard the sound of his body hitting the train. It was a surprisingly small sound, barely audible behind the screech of brakes. It was just a little muffled thud.

Everyone moved. In a fraction of a second the huge body of people seemed to disintegrate and re-form into a new organism. At that moment everyone changed, stepped forward or stepped back, raised arms, turned heads, put their hands on their hearts or in their mouths, and there was an instant kaleidoscope of chaos before we became again a crowd of commuters who had just seen a man go under a train.

I heard all the commotion, but only as a distant, disembodied music. The sound of the background cassette being chewed up. All I really registered was the dull thud with no resonance, and the sound of the black girl's scream.

She looked electric. A space had cleared around her as though people were afraid of getting a shock. Her long fingers were outstretched, and her mouth was wide open. Her face disappeared into a gaping cavern and the scream came out like a hurricane. I thought the tunnel would crumble around us.

The doors of the train remained closed, and the passengers rose with worried expressions. They stared out of the windows at the people on the platform, and the people on the platform stared at the people on the train. The men in uniform, appearing from all directions, moved among the crowd giving instructions and then, slowly, the giant millipede began to crawl back up the stairs.

Daniel once told me, 'When someone dies, the image of the last thing they looked at remains on the retina.'
I shivered.
'If you examine the retina of a corpse,' he said, 'you will see a clear picture of the last thing that person saw.'

She was next to me. She was shaking her hair and biting her lip and glancing at me, so I gave her one of those unsmiling smiles to let her speak.
'He looked me,' she said.
She smelt of plastic and fresh sweat.
'I know,' I told her. 'He looked at me too.'
'Those eyes,' she said. 'Did you see his eyes?'
I didn't want to think about them but I nodded. We were nearly above ground. The City air seemed somehow different, new and cleaner, and when we reached the street I'd forgotten that I'd gone down on my own. Now there were two of us. For a long time we just stood together, breathing.

Fight or Flight

'So remember what I've told you.' The senior consultant rose, indicating that their time was up. 'Your son has his reasons - be patient.'

Bea and Robin hastily put on their coats.

'Thank you so much,' said Bea as the consultant opened the door. 'You really have put my mind at rest.'

She shook his outstretched hand but Robin pushed past her, scowling, and headed for where Tom sat contentedly building plastic brick castles with the receptionist.

'Now then! How's the boy?' Robin grabbed his son from behind and swung him boisterously into the air high above his shoulders. 'What a waste of time! Sorry Tom - we're going home now.'

'Robin!' Bea cringed, aware that the consultant's open door left him easily within earshot, but her husband ignored her.

'What a silly doctor,' he whispered loudly into the child's ear. 'Come on, Tom - we've got much better bricks at home.'

Tom looked longingly over his father's shoulder at the unfinished castle but he did not complain. He waved politely at the receptionist who, obviously enamoured, smiled warmly at Bea.

'What a lovely little boy you have!'

Bea's sharp features softened with relief.

'Thanks. We think so - but you know how biased parents are!'

The receptionist laughed.

'No, in this case you have every right - I see plenty of children in this job but I tell you, I could take that one home with me! Do you know what he just did . . . '

'Bea! Come on!'

Robin was glaring at her, struggling to keep the heavy door of the lift open while balancing Tom on his shoulders, and Bea shrugged apologetically at the receptionist and ran.

'Thanks again!' she called as the lift doors closed.

'For God's sake!' snapped Robin. 'What the fuck are you thanking everyone for?'

Bea sighed and leant against the wall of the lift.

'I feel better - you know, Robin, I really do - just knowing that he's not the only one.'

Robin grunted.

'It doesn't solve anything though, does it?'

He marched out of the lift and through the swing doors into the street, his black leather jacket flapping around his slim body. Bea hurried to catch up and caught the full force of the swing doors which left her winded.

'Will you slow *down*, Robin,' she called. 'Will you just listen for a minute please?'

But Robin was already in the car, fastening Tom in the child-seat and starting the engine.

'What pisses me off most,' Robin said, steering with his elbows as he rolled a cigarette, 'is the fact that I allowed myself to be persuaded to involve the bloody medical profession in the first place.'

Bea watched the road nervously and reached for the tobacco pouch.

'Shall I do that for you?'

Robin swatted at her hand.

'I can manage thank you.'

Bea sank miserably into her seat and braced herself for a collision.

'Bloody doctors,' muttered Robin. 'They just talk up their own arses!'

'Robin - please!' Bea indicated the child who sat silently behind them. 'Language!' she hissed. Robin snorted.

'What do you mean - 'language?'

Bea sighed and ran her hands through her blonde bob.

'You know what I mean, Robin - just be careful.'

'Careful!' Robin screeched to a halt at a red light. 'What the fuck do you mean? What are you talking about?'

He turned to his wife, his mouth slack with contempt.

'What the fuck is there to be careful of? Fuck all!'

His top lip curled. 'Or had you forgotten, Bea? Had you forgotten that our son has never uttered a single word in his whole life?'

Bea added a final seasoning to the minestrone and placed the French loaf in the oven to warm. Then she turned to her son who sat busily arranging the objects on the kitchen table.

'Nearly suppertime, Tom.'

The little boy looked up at her and grinned, the toothy, dimpled smile which Bea had seen melt grown men into babbling imbeciles. That was a smile to conquer nations, she thought, ruffling her son's black curls and giving him a hug.

'Are you going to call Daddy for supper?'

Tom grinned again.

'Go on- call Daddy.' Bea pressed her cheek against his. 'Go on, Tom,' she urged. 'Say it for me - say Daddy. Go on, darling - Daddy, Daddy, Daddy.' The wide brown eyes stared back at her. It was an expression Bea had come to know well and which they now called 'Tom's Look', a watchful silence both knowing and contained.

'It's like he's analysing us,' Bea had laughed. 'God, I hope he's not going to follow in his father's footsteps - living with two psychoanalysts is bound to make me completely neurotic!'

In the beginning Robin had been unperturbed by his son's muteness.

'Absolutely nothing to worry about,' he reassured Bea. 'In fact it's a good sign. You see he's developing an extremely rich inner world.'

Even as a baby Tom had made little noise. He developed an extraordinary manner of soundless crying in which his little shoulders would tremble and shake and huge tears would roll down his cheeks, but his gaping mouth never emitted a single sob.

'Of course, we removed his vocal cords at birth,' Robin joked with their friends. 'Makes them so much easier to live with, don't you think?'

He was proud of his son, who had inherited his handsome Mediterranean looks, and he was fond of telling people how late starters were usually the children who blossomed into geniuses, but when Tom's second birthday passed without a murmur from the boy Robin's confident assertions began to waver. At Tom's third birthday party he watched his best friend's small daughter name every object in the room, count to ten and recite her full name and address, and Bea noticed that later he reprimanded the little girl with quite uncharacteristic severity for spilling her jelly.

'Robin! Supper!'

Bea was grating fresh Parmesan into a bowl as her husband emerged from the study where he had remained since their return from the hospital. He sidled up behind her, placing his hands on her narrow hips and burying his face in her neck. Bea turned and stroked his cheek.

'Okay?'

He nodded.

'Anything I can do?' he asked.

Bea smiled. She had never known her husband to apologise but it did not seem to matter when he was always so blatantly contrite after bitter words. She almost could not bear the guilt in his eyes and his tentative gestures, so different form the confident self-assurance he normally exuded.

'No - it's done - why don't you sit down?'

'Actually - er - ' Robin pushed the thick black hair from his eyes. 'It smells delicious but actually, Bea, I'm not very hungry. I think I'll get off if you don't mind.'

'Already!' Bea glanced at the clock. 'But your group doesn't start until seven.'

'I know - I just feel - ' Robin shrugged. 'Look, Bea, I'll have supper later. I'll just go for a bit of a ride - clear my head.'

Bea sighed and began to spoon soup into Tom's bowl.

'I'll see you later, love,' said Robin, already half-way out of the door.

Bea turned abruptly.

'Wait!' she called. 'Haven't you forgotten something?'

She nodded at Tom.

'Oh yes.'

Robin waved rather feebly at his son.

'Bye, Tom.'

Tom waved his soup spoon obediently.

'Bye, bye, Daddy,' sang Bea.

Robin managed a weak smile and left.

The Norton throbbed effortlessly between Robin's legs. His motorbike had caused a fair amount of marital strife over the past three years but Robin had insisted that Tom's birth, which had precipitated the acquisition of a family Volvo, did not also necessitate the departure of his most beloved possession. This evening he took his favourite route around the Heath and then went for short blast down the North Circular before returning to Hampstead via Alexandra Park. He stopped, as he always did, at Alexandra Palace, to smoke a cigarette and take in the view, and as usual it cheered him to be high above the rest of London, looking down like a god on the myriad of ugly confusions which merged to become, from such a distance, beauty itself. He arrived at the Institute of Psychotherapy with the characteristic serenity for which he was renowned, smoked a final cigarette astride the silent motorbike and shared a joke with a fellow analyst before entering the large Victorian doorway at precisely seven o'clock to lead his group.

They were waiting for him. The six sat quietly on their circle of cushions and the twins, as he called them, greeted his customary 'Good Evening' with the beaming mouths of hungry chicks in a nest. Melanie raised her beautiful eyes to meet his with a furtive smile, and the American woman, as usual, assumed a practical nonchalance which belied her hysterical outburst of the previous week.
'Well, hi, Robin, how ya doing?'
Robin gave a brief nod, slipped out of his leather jacket and sank easily into a cross-legged position on his cushion. He waited. Without focusing on any individual he surveyed the silent group. They were all trainee therapists, in their first year of study, and Robin had to admit that he would be glad when the group ended for the summer. Not that it had been without successes. The twins, for example, had both confronted and worked through an enormous amount of unresolved conflict around their respective mothers. They were not related, and were physically unalike as two men could be, one so big, dark and muscular and the other a pale, hollow-chested fellow, but their reactions and emotions, their absolute text-book behaviour, had been so similar that Robin had joked with a colleague about his desire to write a radical new paper entitled 'The Myth of Individuality.' Naturally the twins both worshipped Robin. They agreed fervently with his every interpretation and tried desperately to emulate his idiosyncratic manner of speech. He noticed, with a mixture of pleasure and disdain that tonight Matthew, the pale twin, was wearing a new pair of suede Doctor Marten boots identical to Robin's own favoured footwear.

Robin glanced over at the other male member of the group. Unlike the sycophantic twins, Graham had always done his utmost to undermine Robin, and for a long time the group had been dominated by his argumentative personality. Now, as Robin looked around,

Graham avoided his eyes and pushed the ginger hair from his freckled forehead. How adolescent in both looks and mannerisms he was, thought Robin, and what a tricky bunch adolescents were, even if this particular one was actually thirty-five years old. But Robin was not worried. He knew that the battle with Graham was drawing to a close, and he noticed that tonight Graham made no attempt to begin the group with his usual aggressive attack. Graham was watching Melanie with a silent, boyish wistfulness that made Robin want to smile, but of course the group analyst kept his face inscrutably composed as he waited.

This evening it was Melanie who finally broke the silence. Pushing her ash-blonde hair thoughtfully from her brow and directing her gaze, as always, straight at Robin, she took a deep, shuddering breath.
'I can't stand this - can't someone say something?'
Matthew, the pale twin, smiled.
'Well you just have!' he declared, looking proudly at Robin. 'It was a longer silence than usual today,' he added knowledgeably.
'Yes,' agreed Robin. 'I would suggest that the prolonged silence indicated our reluctance to address a matter of importance.'
He paused and looked around again but since no-one spoke he continued.
'Some unfinished business from last week perhaps?' He looked pointedly at the American woman.
'Okay, okay.' She held up her hands in a position of surrender. 'Okay, guys - I'm sorry, right? I was out of order last week, I know. I just - well - I just kinda freaked out.' She tugged her frizzy hair and turned to Melanie. 'And I'm especially sorry to you, Mel, I was out of order and I didn't mean to yell at you.' Melanie smiled and nodded.
'It's okay, Joyce, I understand. We all get angry sometimes.'
The two women smiled at each other and the twins looked relieved. Graham looked slightly disappointed, but managed a smile too.
'Hold it,' said Robin.
The smiles vanished.
'That's all very nice,' said Robin. 'But all you've done is avoided the issue.'
Joyce returned her attention to her shoes.
'You can't have your pudding till you've eaten your main course,'

said Robin. He smiled, pleased with the metaphor. Robin had a reputation at The Institute for his astute metaphorical interpretations.

'You've got to eat the whole dinner to get the full nutritional value,' he continued. 'If you can't digest the heavy stuff the sweeties won't do you any good at all.'

Joyce eyed him.

'I don't get you,' she said. 'I just don't get you, Robin.'

'Oh I think you do,' replied Robin.

'I think I see,' said Mark, the dark twin, eagerly. 'You mean we still haven't looked at why the argument started in the first place?' He leaned back in his chair, basking in Robin's cursory nod.

'Well - I - ' Joyce bit her lip. 'I didn't mean to have a go at Melanie - it's just that - '

Robin flashed her his most understanding smile.

'Something this group needs to address is competitiveness,' he announced. 'Competitive jealousy is difficult - it's not an emotion we're comfortable with.'

The group looked at him. Joyce shuffled on her cushion.

'We say we're in this game for the love of playing - no-one wants to admit that they want to win.'

Mark frowned.

'But what are we trying to win, Robin?' he asked. 'What are we playing for? What are we competitive about?'

Robin rolled his eyes in irritation.

'Well,' he replied. 'Perhaps you can tell me.'

Joyce lowered her head. Melanie glanced at her, and then looked at the men who were all watching Joyce remove her large glasses and wipe them slowly on her sleeve. Joyce sniffed and tentatively raised her watery eyes to squint at Melanie.

'It's okay for you, Mel,' she said quietly. 'Everyone likes you 'cos you're so pretty.'

Robin was nodding his head.

Joyce looked around at the barely disguised pity beneath the cultivated expressions of concern.

'It's like this you see,' she told them. 'I've always been like - like the one who nobody looked at - the one who never got the guys.' Her loud voice cracked suddenly into a sob.

'Yes,' said Robin. 'Yes, sexuality could certainly be on the competitive agenda.'

He smiled invitingly.

As Joyce spoke Robin watched the reactions of the rest of the group. Matthew and Mark had assumed identically intent expressions of concentration. Occasionally one or the other would make a comment but Robin knew that they were feigning interest, waiting politely for a chance to prove their analytic powers by a weak imitation of Robin's method of interpretation. Graham was plainly bored as he always was when the attention was focused on someone other than himself, and he occupied his fidgety hands by pulling the hair out of his ears. Melanie sat composed, watching the older woman with a sympathy not quite devoid of pleasure. Unconsciously she stroked the fine bones of her cheek, as if reassuring herself of her natural advantage.

And finally Robin allowed himself, for the first time that evening, to look at the last member of the group.

It was her stillness which always struck him first. And perhaps it was her stillness that allowed him to ignore her, as though she was merely a statue amongst the living, breathing, whimpering circle. She dressed almost always in black, a startling contrast to her smooth white skin, and she kept her abundant dark hair severely restrained with a tight ribbon. There was nothing remarkable about her, Robin thought, but it was Sarah's eyes that got him, those penetrating eyes. As they all listened to Joyce's garbled and confusing memories Robin was very aware that he, too, was being observed.

When Joyce's tears finally stopped it was at Sarah she smiled.

'Oh gee ~ I'm sorry ~ I've done it again haven't I ~ done all the talking.' She screwed up her eyes at the silent woman. 'Hey, you know, Sarah, how comes you always do the listening and never tell us anything about yourself?'

Sarah gave a small, self-deprecatory shrug.

'How do you do it?' Joyce persisted. 'How comes you never share anything with the group?'

Sarah winced slightly.

'I'm sorry,' she said. 'I must admit that I find it very hard to talk in front of so many people. I mean - it's quite scary isn't it?' She looked around, her grey eyes questioning.

'You fascinate me,' continued Joyce. 'You seem so - so above it all.'

'Yes, that's it,' agreed Mark. 'You seem so superior, Sarah.'

Sarah gave a little laugh.

'Oh dear,' she said. 'Perhaps that's my defence, because I certainly don't feel superior. Please understand that I'm hopeless in groups - I'm sorry.'

'Mmm,' said Joyce. 'So you're saying that in some way you don't want to join in'

'No,' replied Sarah. 'What I'm saying is that I'm finding it very difficult to say very much.'

Robin opened his palms to the ceiling.

'But Sarah,' he smiled. 'The group wants to understand you - and words are all we've got.'

She stared at him.

'I disagree,' piped up Graham. 'You're wrong there, Robin. Actually there's a lot more to us than words - expressions, gestures, unconscious processes, you know - surely you've read your Klein, Robin?'

Robin gave him a withering look, glanced at his watch and removed the tobacco pouch from his pocket. He began to roll the cigarette which signalled the imminent end of the group.

'Well - to sum up - this has been a useful session.' Robin nodded at Joyce. 'We're learning to trust more.'

Joyce smiled.

'You see - ' he licked the cigarette paper. 'We've all got a load of dust under our sofas. There's a lot of junk - a lot of shit we push under there, hide it out of the way to sort out later - but of course we never do. It stays there festering. We're embarrassed if someone peeps underneath and sees our mess, but somehow we just can't face pulling out all that mess and sorting through it.'

He tucked his cigarette behind his ear and smiled around the group.

'But now, perhaps, it's time for spring cleaning!'

Matthew and Mark chuckled appreciatively but Robin was already out of the door with his usual parting shot.

'Think on it – see you next week.'

The twins turned to Joyce to offer congratulatory noises while Melanie asked Graham to explain the significance of the sofas, beginning a discussion which continued in the pub until last orders. Only Sarah was missing, slipping away silently before the others even noticed she had gone.

Robin tucked the wooden train set neatly back in its box, poured himself a large whisky, and sat listening to the low murmur of Bea reading Tom's bedtime story. For once he could not get the group out of his head. Robin hated work to follow him home and he picked up a copy of 'Classic Bike' and tried to concentrate on a very appealing photograph of a BSA Gold Star. But there was one face that kept creeping back into his mind. It was odd, he thought, how he could not stop thinking about her. Certainly if the beautifully pouting Melanie had wandered into his thoughts he would not have been in the least surprised, but Sarah was certainly not the sort of woman who generally inhabited Robin's head. He took a long gulp of whisky.

'Robin!' called Bea from the top of the stairs. 'Tom wants you to come and say 'Night-Night'.'

Robin reached for the bottle of Bell's and added another generous splash to his glass.

'Robin!'

'Night-Night, Tom,' he shouted.

'Oh Robin!' called Bea. 'Can't you come up?'

Robin sighed.

'Who's asking?' he shouted back. 'You or Tom?'

There was no answer. He heard Bea go back into Tom's bedroom for a moment, and then the sound of her light foot-steps down the stairs. She popped her head around the door of the living-room.

'Hey, guess what! He's following the words in the book! Honestly, Robin, pointing at the words as I say them.'

'Mmm, great,' muttered Robin without looking up.

Bea clicked her tongue on her teeth, a habit which irritated Robin quite acutely.

'Good group?' she enquired.

'Mmn.'

Bea noticed the half-full tumbler by his arm and frowned.

'Can't have been that good!'

'What?' Robin looked up and Bea nodded curtly at the whisky.

'Oh don't start, Bea.'

Bea merely raised her eyebrows and went back upstairs to run a bath.

'Well, that seminar we've just been to was useless,' complained Graham. 'All that Oedipus complex stuff - I'm surprised you go for all that Freudian drivel, Robin - I thought you were supposed to be so radical.'

Robin crossed his legs.

'This is an experiential group,' he told Graham. 'We're not here to discuss the theoretical seminars. But what I always say is - pick what you want. There's no need to rigidly adhere to specific theories - pick and choose. You'll find they all have a place.'

'It's a load of bollocks,' muttered Graham. 'Desiring the mother, wanting to kill the father, fearing castration - it's all so - so - boring!'

'You seem very angry,' observed Robin.

'I'm just pissed off with wasting my time listening to bullshit,' said Graham.

'Perhaps,' said Robin, 'you are angry about this group too. You are saying the seminar didn't give you what you want - perhaps here, too you feel that you are not getting what you want.'

He stared at Graham.

'Robin's right,' said Melanie gently. 'You're furious about something, Graham.'

Graham clenched his fists.

'Robin's right, Robin's right!' he sneered. 'You think he's got all the answers?' He glared at Melanie. 'Why do you always side with him?'

'I don't,' Melanie began.

'Yes you do!' Graham flushed angrily. 'You believe everything he says like he's a fucking oracle or something - and the way you look at him all the time, it's like - well, it's like . . .'

'Like what, Graham?' asked Robin quietly.

Graham glared him and then looked at the floor.

'Well, it's like she's - in love with you,' he mumbled.

'So,' said Robin. 'You are angry about a perceived relationship between myself and Melanie - a relationship from which you feel excluded - yes, Graham?'

Graham nodded at the floor.

'You think I am in some way preventing you from having Melanie,' continued Robin, 'and so you are determined to put me down, to show me and my theories to be useless, to therefore *destroy* me. Is that not the case?'

Graham folded his hands over his crotch.

'And now,' said Robin, 'look at your hands. I think that now you are aware that I know all this, you are fearing what I will do to you. Well, Graham? Do you think now that I, the bad father, am about to castrate you?'

Graham blushed and half-raised his head to look at Robin. He looked as though he was about to cry. But Robin smiled and nodded encouragingly.

'So there you have that Oedipal bollocks, Graham,' he said gently.

There was a murmur of approval and finally Graham looked up at Robin and grinned.

'Well I can't argue with that I suppose,' he sighed. He glanced nervously at Melanie. 'God it's not easy is it?' he said. 'I feel totally humiliated.'

'It's okay,' said Melanie, reaching out a tiny hand to pat his arm. 'It's okay to feel angry, Graham. I mean, we've all got angry here haven't we? Remember when Matthew and Mark had a real go at each other - in that sibling rivalry thing?'

Everyone laughed and the twins smiled at each other.

'You see we've all been angry or upset with each other,' continued Melanie. 'Except - except Sarah, of course.'

'Yeah, that's right, Mel,' agreed Joyce. 'You're absolutely right - what is it with you, Sarah?'

The two women turned towards Sarah and then, united, looked at Robin.

'So we're talking about anger,' said Robin. 'Think about it - there are many ways of showing anger.'

He could feel Sarah staring at him but he did not look at her.

'You see,' he continued, 'one of the greatest ways of expressing anger is to withhold, to withdraw. Sometimes, you see, you can attack purely by walking in the opposite direction.'

'How's that then?' said Graham. 'I can't see how you can attack by keeping quiet.'

'Well it's hardly your style is it?' said Robin coldly. He checked the time and removed his tobacco pouch. Matthew and Mark looked uncomfortable but did not speak. They eyed Sarah warily. Eventually Melanie put her hand to her forehead.

'So, Robin, you mean Sarah's attacking us by not telling us anything?' But Robin was already putting on his leather jacket.

'Hostility has many disguises,' he said through clenched teeth. 'Think on it. See you next week.'

Bea was already in bed when Robin got home. Half asleep she reached for him when he climbed in, and wrapped her small, child-like body around his legs as he sat up in bed rolling a cigarette. He stroked the back of her neck, and feeling a stab of arousal from the pressure of her naked skin against his thigh, he let his hand wander to her firm little breasts. But the image which sprung into his mind was of a very different body, a large, soft swell under thick black wool, and the white skin of an exposed throat. He was quite unaware of how hard his fingers were squeezing Bea's nipple.

'Ouch!' she murmured. 'Robin, you're hurting me - stop it, I'm tired.' The sound of her voice startled him and Robin felt suddenly ashamed. He was almost relieved when Bea pushed his hand away and turned her back to him.

'I had a dream about the group last night,' announced Matthew. Six pairs of eyes turned to him dutifully.

'We were in a forest,' he explained. 'Robin was on a horse, a big white stallion. And then I realised he was Robin Hood and we were all the Merry Men.'

'Oh yeah?' said Graham unkindly. 'And who was Maid Marion?' Everyone looked at Melanie, who giggled.

'Well the thing was,' Matthew continued, unabashed, 'there we all were, Robin and his band of Merry Men but you, Sarah, you weren't with us, in the band I mean - you were sort of hidden behind the trees.'

'Right!' cried Joyce. 'Well that's just how it is, isn't it? She never shares or joins in - she just watches - right Robin?' Robin did not reply.

'It's a definite attack on the group,' said Mark with a stern glance in Sarah's direction.

'But what can we do?' asked Melanie. 'Anyway, how did Robin Hood get his band all together?'

'Ah!' said Robin. 'You see, here we have it. It's an excellent reference, this Robin Hood because, like him, the group expects me to be all - bountiful. You expect that I can always give to the poor. You must remember, however, that the group analyst is not omnipotent. Perhaps someone is so locked in their persecutory fantasies that they will not allow the group near.'

'But Robin never gave up!' cried Melanie. 'That was what was so great about him - he kept trying.'

Robin smiled at her.

'And so we shall,' he said, turning towards Sarah. 'You see the group seems to think that you, Sarah, are trapped in your own forest, so to speak. And perhaps you expect us, like Robin Hood, to fight through the thickets to reach you.'

Sarah looked slightly appalled.

'Mmm,' she said. 'To tell you the truth, I never quite trusted Robin Hood's motives myself.'

Graham sniggered.

'You see!' Robin threw back his head. 'You see what I mean, Sarah - you are simply stuck in this need of yours to feel persecuted. You are determined not to trust the group.'

Sarah closed her eyes for a moment.

'I *am* trying,' she said. 'But I find it very difficult when the group seems to be telling me that I'm not behaving in the right way.'

'No, no.' Mark rubbed his hands together. 'We're just pointing out why we - er - why we find you - er - difficult.'

'Because you don't seem to like the group,' added Matthew. 'You don't seem to like us, Sarah.'

Sarah looked him.

'I think what you mean,' she said slowly, 'is that you don't like me.'

There was a slight pause before Joyce said loudly,

'Nonsense! What a load of nonsense, Sarah. Of course we like you!'

She looked around. Matthew and Mark nodded violently.

'Of course we like you, Sarah.' Joyce repeated. 'I've always liked you. It's just - well - it's just that at the moment I can't think of anything positive to say about you.'

Sarah raised one eyebrow.

'Oh that's it, is it?' she said, with only the merest trace of irony. 'Oh, I see.'

'He's counting!' said Bea. 'Look, Robin, he's counting in his head.'

She pushed the pile of coins back across the pine table to Tom.

'Watch, Robin!'

Robin reluctantly glanced up from 'The Independent'.

'Four!' cried Bea.

The little boy carefully pushed four coins towards his mother.

'Well done, darling. See, Robin! Did you see that?'

'Not bad at all.' Robin winked at his son and returned his attention to the film reviews.

'Three!' bellowed Bea.

Tom pushed three coins forward.

'Robin!' Bea grabbed at the newspaper and snatched it away. 'Robin! Will you just *look*!'

Robin sighed.

'Yes, love, I know.' His voice dragged with a weary irritation. 'Okay. Our son can count. What do you want me to do? Phone the Prime Minister?'

Bea pursed her lips so tight that her small mouth almost disappeared. Then she flung the newspaper at her husband's feet and marched out. Robin began picking up the scattered sheets as Tom gathered the coins together in a pile. The little boy began banging a coin loudly on the table but Robin opened the reassembled newspaper and kept his eyes firmly on the print.

'If you want my attention,' he told Tom, 'you'll just have to ask.'

The banging persisted.

'Why don't you just say 'Daddy'?' enquired Robin without looking up. 'It's a lot easier, you know.'

The banging stopped.

Robin smiled to himself and waited, but when he finally looked up the child had gone.

'And another thing!' Joyce was saying to Sarah. 'Why can't you talk properly? I can hardly hear what you're saying - you whisper!'

'Yes, that's true,' agreed Melanie. 'You should speak up a bit, Sarah.'
Sarah looked bewildered.
'I'm sorry,' she said. She coughed and cleared her throat. 'I'm sorry.'
Her voice strained, ended in a squeak, and she smiled at her own
effort. 'I didn't realise it was so hard to hear me - you should have
told me before.'
'You're still whispering,' said Joyce huffily.
Robin was finding it increasingly difficult to keep still. His legs
twitched and he rubbed his knees.
'Below the belt!' he announced suddenly.
The group looked at him blankly and for once he forgot what he had
intended to say. He could not even remember why he had been
thinking about boxing in the first place. He coughed.
'Carry on, Sarah,' he said.
Sarah shrugged her shoulders.
'I'm sorry,' she said again. 'I'm in Catch 22 aren't I?'
In an attempt to sound as gentle as possible Robin's voice became
menacingly low.
'Would you like to tell us what you mean?'
Sarah took a deep breath.
'Well,' she said. 'If I don't speak you are angry that I'm not speaking.
When I do speak you say I'm not saying the right things - and if I try
to say the right things you tell me voice is all wrong.'
She looked around, her wide grey eyes seeking acknowledgement
but finding only hostile stares, and turned her gaze to the floor.
'Ah!' said Robin.
Sarah looked up.
'Well there you have it,' said Robin. 'So you are saying, Sarah, that
the group is at fault, the group is bad.'
'No - ' Sarah shook her head. 'I'm not - what I mean is - '
But Robin was not listening.
'You're saying, Sarah, that the group is harming you in some way - I
see.'
He smiled.
'You understand do you, all of you,' he said, making eye contact with
each member in turn. 'You understand that it is possible to win a
battle merely by showing your wounds?'
Matthew and Mark nodded vehemently.

'What battle?' asked Sarah quietly.

'Well obviously the one you're fighting with us, honey,' said Joyce coldly.

'I'm not trying to fight a battle,' sighed Sarah. 'I'm just trying to understand what you mean. And to tell you what *I* mean. And I find your manner of speaking, Robin, quite frightening.'

Robin adopted his most casually relaxed position, leaning back on his cushions with his legs stretched out, feet crossed.

'Perhaps you are now trying to manipulate me into a response, Sarah,' he suggested.

'All I'm trying to do,' replied Sarah, 'is to honestly communicate how I feel.'

For a moment Robin looked as though he had a bad taste in his mouth, but then he smiled around the group. His legs stopped twitching as he folded his hands and listened to the soothing calm of his own voice.

'You see, we're like an orchestra . . . ' he began.

Matthew and Mark watched Robin's every gesture. They hung on his every word, trying to absorb each phrase for future use. Graham's fingers began to delve around in his ear but he looked, for once, as though he was listening to Robin. Joyce placed her chin in her hands where it nodded rhythmically, while Melanie gazed at the group leader if not with total comprehension, at least with the unconditional adoration of a teenager. And Sarah watched them all, her stillness broken only by the slight trembling of her lower lip.

'So perhaps that's why the group analyst is often referred to as the group conductor,' finished Robin. 'I'm like the conductor of the orchestra. I don't play an instrument myself, but I'm here to guide you through the symphony.'

He gave a self-effacing smile. Mark clapped his hands together.

'And we all play different parts, Robin!' he cried. 'We all play a different tune but we fit together, don't we?'

'Jesus!' laughed Joyce. 'What am I playing then? The big bass drum?'

'No, no, you're definitely in the wind section,' giggled Matthew.

'Oh gee, thanks a lot!' Joyce pulled a face but could not help smiling.

'And Graham must be the clashing cymbals,' continued Matthew.

'And I think I'm a violin - sitting next to a cello or a double bass.' He patted Mark's hefty shoulders.

'And me?' asked Melanie eagerly. 'What am I?'

'Oh you're a flute, Mel!' shouted Joyce. 'A sweet, dainty flute.'

'Or a little piccolo,' suggested Mark. 'Or a tinkling triangle.'

They smiled at each other and then, as the laughter faded, their eyes began to fall on Sarah. Robin waited a moment before raising his index finger.

'But has someone, perhaps, forgotten their instrument?' he inquired. 'Or is someone wilfully playing in the wrong key? Indeed, is someone playing an entirely different piece of music in an effort to sabotage our efforts?'

Robin was sure he could see her grey eyes shining with tears.

'Well, Sarah?'

They stared at each other.

'I'm sorry Robin,' she said quietly. 'I know I've said it before - but you misunderstand me.'

Robin raised his eyebrows.

'I'm obviously in the wrong place,' she said sadly. 'To continue your analogy I've never had a music lesson in my life and now I've turned up in the concert hall and been told I've got to play Beethoven's Fifth on a Jew's harp.' She looked straight at Robin and her voice became stronger.

'And there's one more problem,' she said.

With an effort Robin unclenched his fists and smiled.

'Oh yes? And what's that? Do tell us, Sarah.'

'Well,' said Sarah, 'the other problem is that the conductor just doesn't seem happy with his job. Don't get me wrong - I don't mean he can't conduct - I know he's familiar with all the rhythms and tones and harmonies, and he certainly knows how to use his baton. It's just, well, somehow I just get the feeling that perhaps it isn't enough for him - that perhaps he wants to write the music as well.'

She shrugged and stood up.

Robin went rigid.

'Where are you going?'

Sarah moved towards the door. Suddenly her face broke into a smile.

'Good luck with the performance,' she said.

Melanie gasped.

'No, wait, Sarah!' cried Matthew. 'No, don't!' He looked at Robin in horror.

Robin remained stonily composed, surveying the circle.

'Hold it, Sarah!' shouted Joyce. 'Cool it now!'

Sarah could not have looked cooler. Robin was aware that everyone was watching him as she glided towards the door. He held up a hand, like a referee, his face fiercely set. Baring his teeth as he spoke he emphasised each word with a sharp precision.

'Ah, so here we have it.' He felt his heart relax as he began to speak. 'Here we have the example of classic fight or flight.'

Robin pointed a finger at Sarah's back.

'As we can see, this particular technique of self-preservation renders my interpretation quite impotent, but it is important that the rest of us understand that is happening here, that . . . '

But no-one was listening to Robin. As Sarah opened the door Joyce let out a shriek and Graham's mouth drooped open in amazement. For a brief moment Sarah glanced back at Robin, but he would not meet her eyes. He was still talking as she slipped out and closed the door quietly behind her.

Tom flew into his father's arms with his usual display of abundant energy, nearly knocking Robin off balance.

'Thanks, Jessica,' Robin called to the nursery school teacher. 'See you tomorrow.'

'Oh wait a minute,' shouted the pretty young woman above the excited chatter of the class. She routed around in a pile of sugar paper and pulled out a large sheet.

'Here - you must take this - Tom drew this for you.'

Robin held out his hand.

'For me? How do you know?'

Jessica tidied a strand of auburn hair and smiled up at Robin. She fancied him, he could tell, and he knew she was glad of this excuse for a chat. Signalling the other children to quieten down she touched his arm.

'Well, look at it!'

Robin looked at the thick smudges of wax crayon. Of course, it was obvious. The tall figure of a man, black jacket, black hair, legs drawn in a perfect denim blue, big boots.

'It's me!' He turned to his son. 'Is it me, Tom? Is it Daddy?'

The child grinned and grabbed his father's hand, pulling him towards the car.

'It's very good!' yelled Jessica, returning to the noisy cluster. 'Very good for his age you know.'

Robin waved and picked up Tom.

'Who's a clever boy then?'

As they pulled into the drive Tom began fiddling with his seat belt, the intricacies of which always left him squirming with frustration. Robin stopped the car and watched the child wriggling and grunting with impatience. Eventually Tom looked up and pointed at the belt with a commanding air.

'Okay,' said Robin. 'Say "undo it Daddy."'

Tom fumbled with the catch again.

'You know you can't do it,' said Robin, 'and I'm not going to help you until you ask me - go on - ask me.'

Tom glared at him.

'Say "help me please Daddy" or just say "Daddy" or "seat-belt" or just "help." Just say anything for God's sake!'

Tom tugged at the belt.

'Just one word and I'll let you out.'

Tom's breathing quickened and then suddenly stopped.

'Oh don't start that!' Robin took out his tobacco pouch and started rolling.

'That won't help,' he told the red-faced child. 'You won't win that way.'

Tom's face gradually became a bright crimson.

'Right!' Said Robin. 'Enough.'

He lit his cigarette and then leaned towards his son with sudden inspiration.

'Okay. Don't say a word. Shut up, do you hear me? Shut up and be quiet!'

A purple hue began to spread across Tom's cheeks.

Robin's face was pressed close to the boy's own. 'Don't you dare speak! Don't you dare. Shut up! Not a word out of you! Button it!'

He was grinning now, unaware of Bea walking down the driveway. He put his hand firmly over Tom's mouth, and then let his long fingers slip around the child's little neck.

'Shut your face, Tom! Be quiet, will you!'

Bea dropped her shopping and ran towards the car.

'Shut up!' Suddenly Robin was shouting at the top of his voice. 'You arrogant little bastard - I'll show you!' He tightened his hand around the child's throat.

'Shut up! Shut up! Shut up!'

Bea peered through the car window at her blue-faced son.

'What the fuck is going on?' she screamed.

At the sight of his mother Tom let out his lungfuls of air with a splutter. He gasped and coughed, his eyes watering with the effort, but still he did not cry. The great heaving, shuddering sobs which filled the car were coming from Robin.

Seeds

When Lucy found herself pregnant she took to buying litre bottles of gin and rearranging the heaviest furniture in her flat. Each morning on the way to work she jumped down the last steps, increasing the number by one step every day until the stinging soles of her feet brought tears to her eyes. Twelve steps did nothing to dislodge the intruder and thirteen looked ominous for Lucy's own neck. It remained intact. Its intention was obviously to be born.

At work Lucy marvelled at her ability to hold reasonable conversations. She felt as if she were talking to people through a long tunnel. Lucy wondered if anyone had noticed the change in her but her colleagues on the acute psychiatric ward seemed oblivious, and the patients would hardly have noticed if she sprouted another head. It seemed ironic to her that she felt so lonely, given that for the first time in her life she was no longer alone.

On Christmas Eve, during a rare solitary moment in the nursing office, Dan phoned her. Despite the religious timing this was, of course, no immaculate conception, but what she and Dan did together had never seemed to be about breeding. He was an artist, contemptuous of domesticity, and he spent weeks alone in his studio in Wales. Lucy didn't mind. She quite enjoyed missing him. Now Dan's words, two hundred miles away, sounded so close that she felt shivers down her neck as if his hot breath were touching her ear, but her own voice was like that of a distant stranger as she impotently groped for the right phrase.
'What's up?' asked Dan. 'You sound funny.'
But the words strangled each other in Lucy's throat as she stared at the wall.
'I'll be home next week,' he told her. 'Home for New Year.'
'That's good,' said Lucy. 'Dan - I've got something to tell you.'
'Look, the money's running out,' said Dan. 'I'll talk to you when I get back.'

'So,' said Dan the following week. 'What are you going to do?'

Lucy was in bed, the duvet pulled up to her nose.

'It's your decision,' said Dan. 'But of course I'll support you in whatever you decide,'

'I've got an appointment for a termination,' said Lucy. 'Abortion,' she added. It sounded more honest.

He hugged her, so she knew it was the right answer.

'So,' said Annabel. 'What are you going to do?'

'Would you - collect me from the clinic?'

Lucy felt she was owed such a favour, having collected Annabel from the same clinic the year before. Annabel's eyes, however, alerted her to the insensitivity of her request.

'I will - ye-es, of course I will.' Annabel instinctively laid her hands on the large lump that was her second, luckier mistake.

'I'm sorry,' said Lucy. 'It's just Dan - well - he hates that sort of thing, hospitals - you know.'

Annabel raised her eyebrows.

'Such a sensitive artist!' she said sarcastically.

'And I don't want him there,' Lucy added.

'Of course I'll collect you,' said Annabel. 'But it won't be easy for me, Lucy, going back there.'

Lucy looked guiltily at her friend. She had tried to forget Annabel's day, returning to Annabel's house and the room with the flickering pink candles, the room which became in the weeks that followed, a shrine. But Annabel was prone to drama and Lucy only wanted a lift in the car.

Ten women sat in the waiting-room. Lucy furtively scanned the faces for emotion but the averted eyes were set in expressions of nonchalance. The nurse behind the desk methodically filled in forms and called each woman in turn to sign, as the excited voice of the radio announced the birth of the second child of the Duke and Duchess of York.

'You'd think she'd turn that off,' Lucy whispered to the young girl next to her. The girl put down her magazine and stared at Lucy.

'Why?'

She looked about fourteen, with a round child's face under her bleached hair. On her arm was a tattoo saying 'Kevin'.

'I just thought it seemed a bit inappropriate,' said Lucy, embarrassed.

'Oh.'

The girl resumed flicking the pages of her magazine.

Lucy was allocated a room with the tattooed girl and a woman of about forty with a hard face.

'Been here before?' asked the woman as they changed into white surgical gowns.

'No,' relied Lucy, surprised that a second visit could be a possibility.

'It's my third,' said the woman before Lucy had time to return the question. The tattooed girl was struggling to find fastenings on the back slit of her garment.

'It don't do up,' the woman told her. 'Just put your dressing-gown over the top.'

'I ain't got one.' The girl held the back of her gown together and turned to Lucy.

'Have you got a fag?'

'Sorry, I've given up.'

'Here y'are, love.' The hard-faced woman produced a packet of Benson and Hedges from her handbag. 'You're not allowed to smoke in here so lean out of the window – you want one too?' She thrust the packet at Lucy who hesitated and then reached gratefully for a cigarette.

'Thanks – I will.'

'Thought so – you look like one of those who says they've given up and then makes a habit of smoking everyone else's.'

'I'm sorry,' stammered Lucy. 'I'll get you some.'

'Don't worry about, it.'

The woman turned away to open the window. Lucy drew on her cigarette, relishing the bitter smoke in her lungs and the rush of nicotine to her head. She had never really wanted to give up smoking anyway.

'Yeah it's not too bad here,' the hard-faced woman was saying. 'Give you tea and sandwiches afterwards.'

'Does it hurt?' asked the tattooed girl.

'Nah – well a bit when you wake up, like period pains.' She turned to face them.

'Vacuum suction,' she said knowledgeably.

Lucy fought to banish a vision of the Hoover attachments under her sink.

'D'you bleed a lot?' asked the girl.

'Don't worry, love,' said the woman. 'How old are you anyway?'

'Sixteen,' said the girl defensively.

The woman snorted.

'I weren't born yesterday, darling!'

'Well not really, but Kev - he'd be in trouble.'

'Your bloke?'

The girl nodded proudly.

'He was well mad when I told him.'

'I bet he was.'

The girl looked from the woman to Lucy and back again, and then pulled up her gown. She touched the yellowing bruises as though they belonged to someone else.

'Threw me downstairs,' she said with a little nod.

Annabel was late. Lucy sat in the same waiting-room watching the next ten women reading magazines. Twice she went to the toilet to check for blood. There was none, and she wondered if it had really gone. The nurse behind the desk kept looking at her then pointedly eyeing the clock. When Annabel rushed in at last Lucy noticed that all eyes drifted to her bulge.

'Sorry, Lucy, I'm just all over the place at the moment.' Annabel was always all over the place. 'You okay?'

Lucy sat silently in the passenger seat thinking about the dream, a laughing magician dressed in white with a metal wand. She wanted to get home, inspect her body. Annabel drove wildly through London, updating her on the last twenty-four hours.

'So now the bloody house has fallen through because of the surveyor's report, and I've got to be out in two weeks' time.'

Annabel pulled up abruptly in a quiet residential area.

'How are you feeling?'

Lucy thought about it. She had been trying to work out what it was that felt different, and she smiled with sudden recognition.

'I don't feel sick any more.'

Annabel leaned over and took her hand. Lucy looked at Annabel's silver bangles glittering in the sun.

'So this is what happens,' she thought. 'People hold your hand.'

'Are you sure you're okay, Luce?'

'Yes, I'm fine.'

'Well then, I thought we might just pop in here and have a look at this house - I've just got the key from the estate agents.'

Lucy felt she was walking just slightly above the ground. The house was cool and white and smelt of new wood, and she followed Annabel through the hollow rooms, listening to the reassuring sound of her footsteps on the floorboards.

'And this would be the baby's room,' Annabel was saying as they entered the smallest bedroom. 'Mmm. Could be lemon, sunny for a nursery.'

Lucy leaned against the bare wall and listened to Annabel's voice echoing in the still emptiness.

'Sorry Lucy,' said Annabel suddenly. 'Stupid of me.'

'It's okay,' said Lucy, sliding gently down the wall and onto the wood floor with a little thud. 'It's nice. I think I'll just sit here for a while.'

Lucy was planting seeds when Dan arrived that evening, pressing them into little pots of moist compost. She planted columbines, delphiniums and passion flowers, and sealed the trays in plastic freezer bags. Dan looked relieved but he kept glancing at her, nervously, as if he expected something. Lucy held up a strange seed, a tiny black ball with a tuft of orange hair.

'Strelitzia,' she told him. 'A bird-of-paradise. You have to pull off the hair and soak it in water all night, and then it will grow.'

In five years' time the bird-of-paradise would be the tallest plant in her flat, nearly as tall as herself, and it would flower just like an exotic bird with its huge blooms of iridescent orange and midnight blue. Lucy placed the seed in the palm of Dan's hand and watched his thick, paint-stained fingers carefully remove the little tuft of hair.

Later, in bed, as he kissed her, she said suddenly,

'Do I smell of dead baby?'

Dan laughed and held her so tight that she could not speak. Lucy thought that she would probably never say anything again. He did not ask her why she could not sleep but produced a sketch pad, pencils, and taught her how to draw with her eyes closed.

'The secret,' he told her, 'is not to take your pencil off the paper.'

They sat up in bed, taking it in turns.

Dan was trying to draw a newt. He looked like a blind man until he finished, opened his eyes with delight, passed the result to Lucy, and began again. The pile of newts grew in her lap. They were strange, amorphous things, with stunted limbs and one big eye. Dan held up the last one and squinted.

'Well, I reckon if I lose my sight I'll be out of a job,' he laughed. 'Which do you think is best?'

The little, unformed creatures looked to Lucy all exactly the same. She smiled at him and fingered the drawings.

'Can I keep them?' she asked.

Reunion

I was ironing when Chrissy phoned me. It had been a year.

'No! You're joking,' she said. 'Where does the time go?'

I was cool, for about ten seconds, until Chrissy's warm voice flooded out from the receiver and melted the frost on my lips. The year disappeared into an hour's delight of drama and drudgery, tales of love and of pain. Chrissy's life was like a soap opera. My own had only the reassuring predictability of domestic bliss. Contentedly, I curled into the big armchair by the fire, hugging the phone as I traded my last twelve months of marriage, the birth of my son and the traumas of moving house, for more gripping stories of passion and betrayal.

'Come for dinner,' Chrissy said. 'On Saturday. Caro's coming.'

I hesitated, not merely for the time it took me to work out that Peter did not have a match that day.

'How's Caro?' I asked.

Chrissy's voice faltered, faded just slightly as she replied. 'She's fine.' There was suddenly a guarded note in her generous voice.

'Caro's fine,' she said again, the comfort of repetition battling with the tension that crept along the telephone line. I was suddenly aware of the crackle in the receiver, and of how badly I wanted to see Chrissy's face.

'You will come won't you, Ruth? Will Peter come?'

'I'm sure,' I replied. 'I'll check with him but I'm sure it will be fine.'

'Brilliant,' said Chrissy. 'Just the four of us. Just like old times.'

Old times. I replaced the receiver and sank back into the chair. I had a thousand and one things to do before Benny woke up but I remained motionless for a long time, staring at the ceiling on which I conjured up their faces, remembering. It started with Chrissy's mouth. Ten years ago, as I self-consciously entered the enormous university dining-hall, Chrissy's mouth was the first thing I saw. It was big, it was red, and it was smiling at me, and I gratefully slid into the empty seat beside her, hoping no-one had noticed my red-rimmed eyes. I was eighteen and cried when my father left me and my suitcase in the tiny campus bedroom while he drove back one hundred miles to the farm and my family. I sat on the narrow bed with the door shut, listening to the noisy unpacking from neighbouring rooms, the introductions, and the excitement in the strange city voices whose volume I interpreted as confidence, and which filled me with terror. I studied the invitation and directions to the Freshers' Dinner and wished fervently for my father to return with a forgotten item, giving me the opportunity to end my academic career there and then.

So I walked into the dining room, trembling in my blue wool dress which had looked so smart in the farmhouse kitchen but now flinched against the glare of black and white chic and the sparkle of jewellery.

'Hi, I'm Chrissy - you're in our hall aren't you? I saw you arrive.'

She was beautiful. Her bright green eyes and sensuous lips arrested the gaze not because of, but despite, the thickly applied make-up which sought to conventionalise her unique features. There was an allure to Chrissy which was more than the sum of the parts and I knew instantly, as she did not, that her red lips, her glossy mane of chestnut hair her voluptuous cleavage, were immaterial to the magnetism which, by the end of the evening, had attracted a period of attention from every man in the room.

'And this is Caro.' She nodded across the table at a strikingly thin girl with jet black hair and large brown eyes, who was emptying the last of a bottle of wine into her glass. 'She's next door to you in the hall.'

'I'm Ruth,' I said, smiling and extending my hand to the girl who regarded it with an amused expression and stood up. Her tall long-limbed body struck a posture which seemed at once both gawky and elegant.

'Pass us that vino,' she yelled in a broad northern accent to the other end of the table whose occupants hesitated, startled into embarrassed silence before obediently passing their untouched bottle to Caro.

'Cheers!' She grinned at the shocked faces and then filled her glass and Chrissy's.

'Thought we'd better get started quick,' she told me. 'It's to our advantage that they're all too fucking polite to tuck in before the first course.'

She fixed me with her huge eyes, judging my reaction and, taking my frozen smile as approval, filled my glass too.

'Go on, be a devil,' she urged, and flashed me a grin which was both warm and coercive. My choice was there, and I paused only briefly, aware of the disapproving glances from the end of the table, before raising the glass to my lips. I chose my future with that first sip and, though I knew not what that future would hold, I thought that wine had never tasted so good.

Although I never fully understood their motives, I was flattered by the attentions of Chrissy and Caro, and I nestled happily under the wing which afforded me the warmth and security of a new family. They took me shopping, squeezed me into the skimpiest dresses, bleached my mousy hair and spent hours back-combing my new platinum halo. They taught me to hide my rosy cheeks with green moisturisers and matt foundation cream and often, on my desk, would be left little presents of lipsticks and eyeliner which they would urge me to try. My happiest times, I remember, were not at the parties, the balls, and the numerous social events, but in the hours spent beforehand in my bedroom, with Chrissy and Caro as excited as two little girls with a Barbie doll, transforming my reflection into an awesome, unrecognisable siren. Caro called it 'getting ready for battle' and indeed Chrissy and I were her army and proud to be so.

Once, as we marched out of the dingy hall of residence, fuelled with gin, I asked Caro who we were fighting.

'Just the rest of the world,' she replied.

Caro was never beautiful but she knew how to sell herself. She had the natural advantage, of which so many women dream, of being able to eat anything she desired without ever putting on an ounce. She displayed her long legs at all times, wearing the shortest of skirts even in the middle of January, warmed only by the ceaseless burning energy within her. She wore only black, but her hair changed colour every week and, though her face was plain, she used it like a blank canvas, painting with professional precision the features she wanted. What she lacked in hereditary gifts she made up for in her vibrancy and expression: Caro's laugh was the loudest of all, her eyes had always an unrivalled gleam, and the pain, when it came, made her face unbearable to behold.

Caro, Chrissy and Baby Ruth. Like fairy godmothers they transformed me, and like wicked step-mothers they fed me on martinis and gin, taught me to smoke cannabis and popped little pills between my lips.

'Ruthie, you're such a light-weight!' Caro would scream, as I staggered in the street, fell down a flight of stairs, and vomited on the carpet, over my bed and, rarely, in the toilet bowl. Caro's hierarchical classification of her contemporaries was based on boxing terminology and ranged downwards from 'first-class heavy-weight', an honour she rarely bestowed but which, loosely translated, meant being able to endure infinite amounts of self-abuse without any undignified consequences. Much of Caro's time was spent practising and, by anyone's standards but her own, she was a world champion. Chrissy was not far behind, but I was never able to build up anything like their superhuman tolerance for intoxicating substances and frequently I found myself, humiliatingly, carried home by my mentors, an arm draped over each of them, my stilettoed feet dragging along the ground and my lolling head lifting just enough to say those increasingly familiar words, 'I'm really sorry about this, girls. I'm so sorry.'

Caro was academically clever, but contemptuous of work and of those students who had to try. Every month, on the first day of her period, she stayed up all night armed with sixty Marlboro, a jar of Nescafe, and a pile of chocolate bars, and completed all her outstanding work, invariably receiving grade 'A's to which she pretended to be indifferent. For the rest of the time she sneered at my conscientious efforts and at Chrissy's sporadic struggles, loitering in our rooms and distracting us until we gave up and joined her for a drink.
'There's much better things to study,' Caro was fond of saying. 'Men for example.'

Men. Nothing in my previous experience had prepared me for the enormity of the challenge before us. I had had boyfriends certainly but the little knowledge of romance that I had acquired was superfluous to the single-minded fervour with which Caro and

Chrissy attacked half the human race. The war waged was called 'beating them at their own game', and we fought with a zeal worthy of Don Juan. The metaphorical notches on the bedpost became a reality when Caro acquired a small saw, but even this was not evidence enough. It was agreed that our conquests should be measured and charted, 'for the purpose of intimidation', said Caro. Chrissy, who was studying mathematics, produced an impressively meticulous graph of the most vital statistics of the male visitors to our rooms, and these plotted penile points were displayed on the noticeboard of our hall of residence, along with calculated averages and a normal distribution curve. But if intimidation was the aim, then we failed in our purpose, for the young men delighted in this audacious homage to their members, and did all but queue up and beg in their eagerness to be immortalised by statistical technique. Only a few never returned.

Caro had a penchant for slim, almost feminine boys, whereas Chrissy's taste veered towards the athletic, muscular types, but they were not rigid in their preferences and frequently shared their partners, although never at the same time. Some things, thankfully, remained taboo. There was no jealousy between them and they worked as a team offering, by virtue of their physical differences, a complete menu to suit all tastes. Sitting in the university bar they would award marks out of ten as each male walked through the door, setting their targets for the evening. Later, with brazen confidence, they would descend upon either side of the chosen victim, two pairs of hands boldly doubling the pleasure of one. I never saw a man immune to these tactics. Embarrassed they may have been, but there was never any lack of delight on the blushing faces which, with whispering from either side and a tongue teasing each ear, would eagerly comply with whatever demands were made. The routine was well known but never failed to attract the horror of other women present, and the envious disdain of the men who secretly longed for such treatment themselves. If the man in question had a preference for Chrissy's buxom charms or for Caro's boyish, almost pre-pubescent body, they rarely let it show, but allowed themselves to be escorted home by whichever had been previously allocated to test out the prize. The other would remain, usually ending up with the company of a previous conquest. The following morning post-mortems were held and the performance of the victim carefully dissected amidst screams of laughter. These morning inquests I attended eagerly, perched on the end of Caro's bed in the smoky half-light, the curtains never opening until their faces were reassembled for the next onslaught. But, although I could not resist the titillating revelations, I would dread the time when the attention focused on my own exploits, and it was not without a sense of betrayal that the details were squeezed out of me.

I fell in love. While Chrissy and Caro pursued the art of surpassing the concupiscence of the male sex, I without fail, became emotionally entangled with every object of lust that crossed my path. First there was Dan, whose boyish good looks and never-ending legs had already been savoured by Chrissy, and in whose arms I lay for the better part of one spring term.

'Ruthie's got it bad,' Caro would say, frowning and shaking her head when I refused to party.

'And all for one so small,' giggled Chrissy who was fond, in Dan's presence, of explaining the inverse relationship between length of leg and length of member. Sadly for me, perhaps, I never learned to appreciate the importance of appendage size, and nor was I in the slightest bit perturbed by what Chrissy referred to as 'Dan's problem'. Premature ejaculation was, for me, the sincerest form of compliment, and Dan was soon the centre of my universe.

Unfortunately, as Chrissy and Caro warned and later, without any hint of smugness, reminded me as I cried on their shoulders, total devotion to a man is as much an aphrodisiac as halitosis. Dan was a free spirit, a follower of the Beat poets, and an incorrigible womaniser.

'Don't lay the guilt trip on me,' he would say. 'Why can't you be more like Chrissy and Caro?'

But as far as Chrissy and Caro were concerned, I never really made the grade.

After Dan there was Rick, and then Rufus, and then many more, each of whom I loved with a loyalty that never learned its lesson. And then there was Peter.

'Do you think Belinda will baby-sit on Saturday night?' I asked Peter on his return from work.

'I should think so,' he replied. 'Where are we going?'

'Chrissy's,' I replied, watching his face. 'Dinner with Chrissy and Caro.'

His expression was indecipherable. There was surprise and there was pleasure, and there was something that made him swallow rather quickly before saying, 'Oh.'

'Don't you want to go?' I asked.

He looked puzzled and began tuning the radio. His voice seemed to become distant.

'Why should I not want to go?'

I regretted my question, but with sudden insecurity I desperately needed to see his face. I went and put my arms around his waist, turning him around.

'It's just you looked - funny.'

He faced me. For a moment I thought we would talk about them.

'Funny?'

Then his face closed again, the moment passed and I said, 'Oh, maybe I imagined it.'

'Perhaps it's you that doesn't want to go,' said Peter.

Peter had the misfortune to fall in love with Chrissy. He was a big man with an impressive physique and, so we learned form Chrissy early on, had qualities down below which led to a raucous discussion as to the relative importance of length and girth. Peter had a warm heart and an extraordinary ugly face. He was fond of relating the story of how his mother used to place him face down in the pram because she was so embarrassed by his repulsiveness. His head was very square, and his face was very squashed, but no-one actually found Peter repulsive. Probably in order to combat these deficiencies he had developed an enormous amount of charm and irresistible wit. He was kind; he was tolerant and, for once, Chrissy broke all her own rules and settled into monogamy for well over three months. Peter drove her around in his old Escort van, he bought her presents, and he served her strawberries for breakfast. Caro looked concerned, but even she never said a word against Peter, perhaps because we had never seen Chrissy look so happy. At that time I was with Rufus, who was actually in love with Caro, but needed a period of distraction from his long-term unrequited passion. He was a small Jewish intellectual who would later be something of a star on Radio 4, and we made an unlikely foursome for dates, sometimes, with Peter and Chrissy.

'She'll break his heart,' said Rufus to me, confidently. I think he happily anticipated seeing Peter reduced to his own humiliating state of rejection. Rufus was usually right, and one night Chrissy disappeared after a party and we found Peter still drunk the next morning, slumped at the wheel of his van. When Chrissy returned she was pale, and for once, unwilling to divulge her whereabouts. She merely muttered something about leaving her best knickers on the snooker table, before disappearing into her room. Eventually, she let Caro in and when, many hours later, they emerged, Chrissy looked as though she had been through a religious conversion; her smile had that static quality.

And then there was Peter and Caro. It was probably Peter who first saw Caro cry, even before we realised that anything was wrong. As finals loomed Caro became louder, drunker, and even Chrissy found it hard to keep up with her insatiable hunger for outrage. I remember one of the last parties when Caro, her hair dyed a startling shade of canary yellow, was holding forth before a male audience on the subject of cunnilingus. She always saw it as her duty to give detailed instruction whenever possible and, although she despised the earnest followers and didactic language of feminism, I felt her monologues did much to benefit the welfare of her sisters. The hostess, a bare-footed daughter of a famous film director, who lived mainly on the weight of her surname, had spent much of the evening glaring at Caro and at the interest she was stimulating in her boyfriend. Eventually, unable to bear the injustice of what she obviously saw as the stealing of her rightful glory, she stalked over to the group, tossing her hair from her face to shamelessly reveal a cluster of acne on her forehead. She stood on the edge of the group of kneeling men, as usual waiting for the mere presence of her surname to silence. Caro ignored her.

'You see the problem,' she was saying. 'The problem is that the textbook fanny is a scientific fantasy created by male doctors who equate sex with simple car maintenance. Press a button - you get a response.'

The hostess's boyfriend seemed unaware of her approach. He was lying on the floor at Caro's feet, laughing excitedly, his hand unconsciously gripping his crotch.

'Oh come on, Caro,' he cried. 'That's unfair. Those kind of books are useful - I mean, a lot of men need a bit of anatomical guidance when it comes to making love.'

'Making love!' Caro spat out the words in disgust. 'Making love! Doesn't anyone realise that love cannot be made? How presumptuous of man to think he can create such a noble emotion purely by carrying out a series of tactile manoeuvres.'

The hostess seized her opportunity.

'How interesting,' she said. 'How interesting, Caro, that one so disparaging of making love should spend so much of one's time engaged in the act.'

She smiled round the group of men, confident of her superior stroke. The sparkle vanished from Caro's face. In a second her expression became uncharacteristically serious.

'I don't make love,' she said slowly, fixing her brown eyes on the hostess. 'I fuck.'

There was a pause, just long enough for everyone's stomach to lurch upwards and back down again, before the hostess reinstated her smile and said, 'Your problem, darling, is that you've just got no class.'

'Class is crass, darling,' replied Caro and left, as it emerged later, with the hostess's boyfriend.

I do not know why I saw that party as a turning point, but perhaps it was to so with the intensity in Caro's eyes which never seemed to leave after that night. Although her behaviour remained predictably outlandish, there was something different, a sense that the preliminary game was over, and that now her battle was for real. But even the spoils of war no longer seemed to give Caro pleasure. Often she would return home alone, smashing milk bottles on her way, and screaming abuse at anyone who tried to stop her. It was only Peter who dared to remove the gin bottle from her lips, who held her arms firmly behind her back as she threw bricks at the vice-chancellor's window, and who finally drove her to the hospital when we found her, delirious in a bed full of empty pill boxes, still clutching the neck of an empty bottle of Gordon's gin. Though I flinched at the blood on the sheets, more horrific was the agony which contorted Caro's face. 'You can't beat them,' she was moaning, as we climbed through her bedroom window. 'You'll never beat the bastards.' When we visited her in hospital the next day, Caro's face was devoid of make-up and expression. Walking into the ward I recognised only her hair, then a vibrant shade of cyclamen, which was spread around her oddly translucent skin. The hair dye had rubbed off onto the crisp white hospital pillow, leaving a pink aura around her head. It was the only time I ever heard Caro apologise, to the brusque nurses who eyed her with uncomprehending contempt as they changed her pillow case. We took her home and fed her Heinz tomato soup, but no-one ever talked about what had happened.

The fear in Caro's eyes that plainly said, 'Don't mention it,' precluded our attempts to understand, and enhanced our own fear of what would happen if we did.

Caro became silent, and embarked on a condensed programme of study, locking herself in her bedroom for three weeks and gaining a first-class degree, to the uncharitable distress of both her contemporaries and her tutors. There was an unspoken feeling that things would never be the same again and it was not without regret that we relinquished our precarious lifestyle and our recalcitrant heroine. Chrissy took it hardest, spending her last days at the university in an inebriated misery, summoning up only enough energy to conceive a child. It was in this atmosphere that Peter and I finally came together, not in the passionate spontaneity in which I'd been instructed, but in the comfortable companionship of shared experience. The outside world seemed an awesome challenge after our bizarre hedonistic existence, and Peter and I gratefully joined forces to meet the future. Chrissy, her Catholic upbringing at last winning its influence, cancelled her abortion and her career, and opted for the long harsh struggle of bringing up a child alone. And Caro finally let her hair return to its natural shade of mouse. She took a series of jobs working with a variety of society's outcasts, and usually refused all social invitations.

As we approached Chrissy's flat on Saturday my mouth felt dry. The rain splashed on the windscreen as Peter drove, and I sat very low in the passenger seat and tried not to think, wishing I could stay forever in motion watching the windscreen wipers. When we arrived it seemed that we both paused just too long at the door, and looked at each other before Peter pressed the bell and we heard Chrissy's frantic footsteps down the hall. She flung open the door and squealed, kissing us both and digging her fingers fiercely into my flesh as she squeezed my arm.

'You're late, you bastards,' she laughed. 'I thought you weren't coming.'

Her green eyes were as bright as ever, her hair even more lustrous, and the lines around her eyes and mouth added a striking drama to her face. They were the lines of the hardship of a single parent but they were also the curves of life. Her smile, always so broad, now had a new depth, a permanence ingrained into her skin.

'I'm so glad you're here.'

'Chrissy, you look fantastic!' I returned her squeeze and she snorted and pulled a face.

'Oh yeah? How do you like my wrinkles?'

'Great stuff,' laughed Peter, pretending to examine Chrissy's eyes. 'Are they a new fashion accessory?'

Chrissy howled. 'Oh Peter, you're such a sweet talker. If you're really good I'll show you my cellulite later! Come on in - Caro's here.'

She was curled in an armchair, holding a glass of wine, and she took another sip before languidly unfolding her long legs as she rose to greet us. She wore a short black dress and her hair was scraped severely from her perfectly painted face.

'Hi guys,' she said.

Although she was now standing, she made no attempt to approach us, and the gesture of rising seemed oddly formal. She was smiling, not at us, but at the embarrassing silence which lay between us.

'How are you, Caro?' It was Peter who finally found the words.

'Fine. And yourself?' There was an ironic tone to her voice and her usually fluid features were composed into a stiff mask.

'Fine.'

'And you, Ruth?' She turned to me with the same mocking politeness and I felt a moment of panic before Chrissy butted in.

'Oh for God's sake, sit down you lot - what do you think this is - a fucking cocktail party?'

She was laughing, but I saw her glance at Caro who seemed to suddenly abandon whatever game she was playing, flopping back into her chair. Her face lost its rigidity and became an open infectious smile.

'Hey, you'll never guess what?' she began. 'You'll never, ever guess who it was!'

'Oh God!' Peter feigned disinterest at her devilish excitement, but his relief at the change in Caro was evident.

'Go on, guess!'

'No,' said Peter. 'Tell us, Caro. You will in the end anyway.'

'Rufus!'

Chrissy laughed delightedly.

'Can you believe it - after all these years,' she said. 'He must have thought it was his birthday.'

'How?' I asked. 'I didn't know you still saw him.'

'I don't,' replied Caro. 'But I just bumped into him in town the other day and he took me out for dinner. You know, all that money he's raking in from the BBC has made him quite flash. So there we were, sloshed and sentimental about the old days, and he said, over the armagnac, 'Caro, let's make love!'

She screamed with glee and launched into a painfully accurate impersonation of Rufus, his accent, his gestures and his neuroses condensed into a supremely funny bedroom farce which had all of us, despite ourselves, rolling with laughter at the intimate misfortunes of an old friend.

'But really,' she finished, 'I suppose it's bad enough having part of your dick chopped off at birth, but there's no need to be so precious with it. He said, 'Caro, Caro. It's not your fault', and I said, 'Damn right it's not my fault,' and kicked him out of the bed!'

'Oh God, poor Rufus,' I said, through tears of laughter.

'Poor Rufus nothing,' retorted Caro, her face suddenly bitter and the humour instantly vanished from the room. Her face resumed the brittle mask which she had displayed on our arrival.

'Poor Caro,' she said. The tone made me catch my breath, and hold it, until Peter spoke.

'Now come on, Caro,' he said. 'Given that last little monologue, you can't say you didn't derive a certain amount of pleasure from the experience.' His voice was gentle but firm. It was the voice he reserved for Caro and she looked up at him, her face once again breaking into a warm smile.

'Why didn't I marry you, Peter?' she asked, not as a question, but as a compliment.

She turned to me.

'Why didn't I marry Peter?' she said.

I could not tell what was behind her smile. It was the same tone of voice that she used to use to make me feel special - 'Oh Ruthie, why haven't I got your hair, your figure, your eyelashes?' It made me feel better, but at the same time I always had the impression that Caro would rather have died than have such a thing.

'You're a lucky girl,' she said now, the shake of her head implying that I had actually suffered some dreadful misfortune.

I looked at my husband, wondering what he was thinking. I was acutely aware of the fact that Peter had carnal knowledge of all three women in the room, and I also knew that Chrissy and Caro would be thinking the same. Although I had no idea what importance Peter placed on this, I was sure that it must at least have crossed his mind. Caro was still staring at me, waiting for my response.

'Is it time for dinner?' I asked.

The meal was slow and delicious. Afterwards we sat for a long time around the table, drinking and reminiscing. The wine soothed my lingering feelings of apprehension and Caro seemed relaxed, keeping us entertained with a steady flow of risqué anecdotes. What happened next seemed, at the time, to occur without warning but, looking back, perhaps we all knew what was on the agenda. One minute I was sitting at the dinner table with Peter, Chrissy and Caro. The next moment there was only Chrissy, and I realised in the instant that I noticed the absence, that I was also very drunk. I do not remember who left first, or even if excuses were made, but I remember Chrissy's frightened face as, leaving her in mid-sentence, I stood up and headed for the bathroom.

Caro was sitting on the toilet and Peter was standing over her.

Though they were both fully clothed, their position formed the most obscene picture I could ever imagine, and the guilt in Peter's eyes, as he turned his head to me, confirmed the obscenity. They did not move, and I think I blinked as though photographing some absurd tableau, before returning in slow motion to the dining room. I could not allow the grotesque image frozen on my retina to pass into my brain as I said a calm goodbye to Chrissy and thanked her for the evening. Peter quickly joined me and there were no farewell kisses nor any need, it seemed, of explanations for our hasty departure. Caro did not reappear.

In the car, as the picture began to seep into the consciousness of my sodden mind, I began to cry. It was a long time before Peter spoke.
'She's like a drug,' he said at last, his eyes firmly fixed on the road.
I managed a little sour noise in contempt of the cliché, blew my nose, and waited.
'She's like drinking too much whisky. It's warm. At first it makes you feel you're special, more special than anyone, because of the desire you believe belongs only to you.'
He looked at me.
'And then it makes you sick. It leaves you sick and shaking and makes your head throb. And you realise you weren't special at all.'
'But you never remember the hangover,' I said bitterly. 'Once you recover you'll accept the next drink that's offered.'
He smiled and did not reply.
'I used to want to be like Caro,' I said. 'Perhaps I still do.'
'Part of all of us wants to be like Caro,' said Peter. 'But she has no place in our lives now. She has nothing to do with you and me, with Benny, with - us.'
I wondered if we kept saying it, whether it would become true.
'We won't see her again,' said Peter.
I watched the windscreen wipers, willing them inside my head to nullify the image which had finally penetrated to become the deepest, indelible memory.
'No,' I said. 'We'll try not to see her again.'

Reasons

Lewis didn't look like he was dying. Apart from the plastic tube forcing an unnatural grimace at the side of his beautiful mouth Lewis looked much the same. Clare slipped into the chair by the bed and let her breathing slow to the rhythm of the ventilator.

Clunk. Ssss. Clunk. Ssss.

He looked very small under the bedclothes. Clare had always loved Lewis' compact little body. She used to be able to lift him up and swing him round, like a child. Now she put her hand out to touch him but hesitated, wary of disturbing the wires from the electrodes on his chest. There was an arterial line in the wrist, and a catheter tube peeped from the bottom of the bed. People had been messing about with Lewis' body and Clare wasn't sure if she was allowed to touch him anymore. So she just sat and watched the stillness of his long eyelashes and listened to his mechanical breathing.

Clunk. Ssss, Clunk. Ssss.

'He wouldn't think much of the outfit!'

Lewis' sister was standing at the doorway shaking her head.

'He always hated white - said it reminded him of his sins.'

Clare looked at the surgical gown and smiled.

'Come on then, Lorna - let's get him into his leather trousers before the doctors come back. Dare you!'

Lorna came towards her, laughing a little too loudly as she caught Clare in a fierce embrace.

'I'm so glad you're here, Clare. I hate it on my own.'

Clare squeezed her.

'Yes - that's what it's like, isn't it? Being on your own - it's like he's not here. Sit down, Lorna - I'll get another chair.'

When she returned Lorna was leaning forwards, her elbows on her knees and hands folded under her chin. Clare watched her studying the brother who was so like her. Lorna wore her thick black hair loose, and Lewis always kept his head shaved, but they shared the same fine bones, strong noses and wonderful dark eyes.

'You look so alike.' She realised that she had never said it before.

Lorna sniffed.

'He got a better deal on the eyelashes,' she said, taking Clare's hand. 'Mum's coming later. They've asked her about - about switching off the machine. The doctor said there was nothing more . . . ' She bit her lip. 'Do you think he can hear us, Clare? Do you think he knows we're here?' Not waiting for a reply she sighed. 'All the times I cursed him, wished he wasn't my brother.'

'Don't,' said Clare. 'No-one's ever happy with their brothers and sisters. That's the whole point of siblings - to teach you about hatred. Don't torture yourself.'

'Did you hate your sister?' asked Lorna. 'Did you ever want her dead?'

'Of course. I would've traded her in a thousand times. I wanted a brother you see.'

'Yes,' said Lorna. 'I suppose I did too.'

They looked at Lewis.

'Do you remember,' asked Lorna, 'when Princess Anne married Mark Phillips? Lewis was about eleven. You know he spent two whole days afterwards in his bedroom making an exact replica of her wedding dress. You should've seen it - it was perfect. And do you know what I did?

'Ssh,' said Clare. 'It doesn't matter now.'

'But it does,' said Lorna. 'It does matter, Clare. You know what I did? I ripped up that bloody beautiful dress. I threw the bits out of the window into the garden, and then I went out and stamped them into the mud. I just couldn't handle it. I just wanted Lewis to be - to be normal.'

Clare shrugged. She knew the story.

'And the worst part,' continued Lorna, 'was that he forgave me. Any other brother would've kicked the shit out of me, but not Lewis. You know what he said? Eleven years old and he says - 'I'm sorry you find me difficult, Lorna."

She burst into tears.

After Lorna had left Clare closed the door and tried to remember all the things she wanted to say to Lewis. What had made her laugh out loud on the underground and what had woken her up in the middle of the night. But somehow it was hard to begin. It was hard to know what was important, the way it always was with Lewis. She thought about Lorna destroying his dress and smiled. Of course Lewis hadn't been angry. Even when his creations began to sell for hundreds of pounds Lewis never seemed to understand that all the fuss was about. 'After all, darling, they're only clothes,' he used to say.

Clare pulled her chair a little closer to the bed and cleared her throat. Then she stood up and began to pull out the dead daffodils from an arrangement of spring blooms. She picked up the card in the centre and read, 'To Dearest Lewis, from Adrian, Saul and Gita'. She did not recognise the names, but whoever they were they obviously had no idea about Lewis' taste in flowers. She looked at her own gift, a single bird-of-paradise on the bedside cabinet. Lewis would have liked that. With a shock she realised that she was thinking in the past tense.

Michael knocked on the door very gently, which irritated Clare, as did the cautious quiet with which he crept up to the bed.

'How is he?' he whispered.

'Oh, on top of the world!'

She didn't mean to snap, and the hurt in Michael's pale eyes made her feel like a prize bitch.

'I'm sorry,' she said, 'it's just . . . '

'I know - stupid question.'

'How are *you*?'

'Okay - well, I'd be a lot better if my best friend wasn't lying there unconscious, but you know how it is. And you?'

'Yes,' said Clare slowly. 'Yes - your best friend. It's funny - I kind of always thought of Lewis as being my best friend too. I told him everything you know. He knew - he knows - more about me than anyone in the world. That's what a best friend is, isn't it - someone you tell everything to?'

'Best friend,' mused Michael, sitting next to her. 'He would hate that term, wouldn't he?'

'Mmm.'

Clare watched Michael watching Lewis.

'It's strange,' she said. 'Often I find myself thinking Lewis would like this, Lewis wouldn't like that. And most of the time I realise I really haven't got a clue. I just want him to wake up so I can ask him. So I can ask him if he's got a best friend, and what his favourite flower is, and who the hell are Adrian, Saul and Gita.'

'Who?'

'They sent those flowers.' Clare pointed out their gift amongst the array of bouquets. 'Do you know them?'

Michael shook his head.

'Lewis knows a lot of people. He has a lot of friends - a lot of best friends.' He hesitated.

'Did he - did he have a lover? Do you know?'

Clare saw that he was embarrassed.

'I think there was someone.'

Michael gave a small smile.

'We never talked about it - after he told me, you know. We just never discussed his relationships. He always said his love life was a disaster.'

'There are two types of men in the world,' quoted Clare. 'Those who I fancy - and those who fancy me.'

Michael laughed.

'Yes, that's it.'

'He was too fond of clichés,' said Clare. 'I said that to him once and he said 'Clare, darling, I don't *use* clichés - I *am* a cliché.''

Michael smiled.

'I was shocked, you know, when he first told me. We were only about sixteen and at that age it's more important to be the same as everyone else. But then Lewis always made a point of being different. He was the first boy in our year at school to have his ear pierced - and then, being Lewis, he had seven rings put in and nearly got expelled for the stud in his nose.'

'They never saw his nipples?'

Michael grinned, shaking his head.

'He always had lots of girls around him, but he just never seemed interested. In their bodies I mean. He was interested in their minds. He'd stay up all night with them chatting - as you said, people always tell him everything. But that was as far as it went. And the irony of it was all the rest of us were just trying our hardest to get these girls into bed - and all the girls wanted was Lewis.'

'Women love him.'

'I love him too, Clare.'

'I know.'

Alone again with Lewis, Clare wondered how much Michael really knew. Lewis told different stories to different people. She had always told him to be careful. It was the only thing she ever told Lewis to do, even knowing that it was the most useless bit of advice to give him. For when he saw the sign in the road saying 'Slow', Lewis just always had to hit the accelerator. Going for a drive with Lewis was the best way Clare knew of cheering herself up - afterwards it always seemed such a miracle that she was still alive. Lewis fixed the strongest Margaritas, rolled the most stupefying joints, and handed you a line of coke that would keep you just about touching the ceiling until the next morning. And he smoked Players untipped, constantly, reverently. He used to say smoking was the most elegant form of suicide. So it was pointless, after all, telling Lewis to be careful. Clare felt a little sob slip out, just as Lewis' lover walked into the room.

He wasn't what she'd expected, but then they never were. It was just she'd never quite given up the idea of seeing Lewis settle into the acceptable face of homosexual monogamy, coupled with a similar bright and articulate young man with a sensitive disposition and artistic leanings. The reality of Lewis' sexual life, therefore, was bound to be a disappointment. Lewis' men were brutes. She was even a little surprised that he was here at all, this huge, leather-clad monstrosity with the blank eyes.
'Hello, I'm Clare.' She held out her hand. He took it briefly, reluctantly. There was no flicker of recognition at her name. Of course Lewis would not have talked of her, even mentioned her. As his large, cold hand dropped hers she noticed that his fingernails were filthy, and she covered her distaste with a smile.
'I'm a friend,' she said.
The grunt of acknowledgement seemed like quite a favour.
'Are you - Sam?'
'Tony.'
She knew it had been an optimistic guess. Sam had been last month.
'Well - ' She rubbed her hands together. 'I was just popping out for a cigarette - I'll leave you alone for a while.'
Tony looked at her. For a moment she wondered exactly how much he had hurt Lewis.

Walking down the long hospital corridor Clare could almost hear

115

Lewis' voice.

'I'm waiting to fall in love. All my life I've been waiting to fall in love. But I'm not half enjoying the dress rehearsals!'

They had been having a picnic in Hyde Park, watching a group of young men playing football.

'Don't fancy yours much,' Lewis told her, indicating the fat youth in goal.

'Mine's the Adonis in the lycra shorts.'

The Adonis in lycra accidentally kicked the ball at Lewis, who promptly sat on it until he came running up. He stopped several feet away, eyeing the ice bucket with suspicion.

'Gisit mate.'

'Of course,' said Lewis. 'But first let me invite you to join my friend and I in a glass of Chablis and perhaps a little snack. We have some rather tasty lobster claws here and - .'

'Nah fanks,' said the young man amiably. 'Can't stand fish.'

'Just an aperitif then?'

'What?'

'A drink?'

'Don't drink wine, mate. Can I have me ball now?'

Lewis sighed, threw the ball and watched the long brown legs running off.

'Another great love affair aborted,' he moaned.

Clare snorted.

'Oh come on! He was a bit young - and a bit short on brain cells.'

'Brain cells! What use have I for brain cells?' cried Lewis. 'I was hardly envisaging a discussion of Schopenhauer.'

'Well, what did you have in mind?'

'Ah, you know.' Lewis stretched out on his back and put on his Ray-Bans. 'Swinging from the chandelier, naked, my legs wrapped around his waist - that sort of thing.'

As Clare walked into the tiny hospital garden she had a sudden vision of Tony's bulk swinging naked from a chandelier, and she burst out laughing. There was a man sitting on the only bench, smoking, and she tried to avoid his eyes as she slipped onto the end of the seat and pulled out her Silk Cut. Keeping her eyes downwards she noticed he was wearing white socks. Lewis hated white socks. He always said they were the one thing that would drive him to homicide. The thought made Clare begin to giggle again.

'Something's tickled you hasn't it?'

She looked up, irritated, hoping she could quash any attempt at companionship with a glare. She wanted to smoke in silence and think about Lewis.

'Share the joke?'

His face was young, eager, like a friendly puppy, and he wore a red ribbon pinned to his lapel. Clare felt like a bull about to charge. 'It's not his fault,' she told herself. She took a deep breath, smiled apologetically, and stood up.

'Sorry, did I say something wrong?'

Not trusting herself to speak Clare headed back indoors, aware of his bemused expression. She checked the Ladies' for smoke detectors and then locked herself in a cubicle, sat on the lid of the toilet, and lit up.

It was kind of funny, she thought, meeting the rest of Lewis' life. It had been a long time since Lewis had let people visit him at home, and so his family and friends rarely met. He'd told her she was the last one to see inside his flat, and she felt this to be quite an honour. She remembered the last time she went there, pushing through the waist high mountains of newspapers, discarded designs, mouldy expresso cups and take-away cartons, and, by a series of complicated manoeuvres and jumps, had reached the only vacant space in the large apartment. Here they lay, surrounded by the sea of debris, marooned on Lewis' bed all afternoon drinking malt whisky. Around the bed a dozen more bottles stood, filled with a similarly coloured liquid. Lewis had explained that it was getting too difficult to navigate his way to the toilet in the night. After that, whenever she asked him about the flat he told it was even worse.

'If you thought it was bad then . . . '

'I should see it now?'

'I'm afraid not. Not even you, Clare, could tolerate the squalor in which I stagnate.'

'Why?' she often asked him.

'Who knows?' he always replied.

It was, perhaps, odd that everyone accepted it. It just became common knowledge that Lewis did not receive visitors. That he lived in somewhat eccentric circumstances. As you might expect of a genius. And Lewis loved to take people out, to spoil them. He never answered the phone, but if you left a message on his machine you would invariably, a few days later, receive one of his little pink cards with an invitation to lunch at The Savoy, or cocktails at The Hilton. Lewis never seemed to realise that people just wanted to talk to him.

'Is someone smoking in there?'
Clare dropped her cigarette into the toilet and flushed the chain. There was a loud banging on the door.
'Hello in there. Are you smoking? Smoking is not permitted in any part of the hospital.'
The banging continued.
'Hello in there. Can you hear me?'
Clare opened the door. She wondered what Lewis would have said to this buxom, moustachioed nurse. She would have loved him. He would have had her giggling like a teenager in minutes. Clare felt the tears coming.
'Leave me alone,' she said, pushing past the nurse as she ran out of the toilets.

She did not want to face Tony again so she went back to the garden. But the man with the white socks was still sitting there. He looked at her peering through the glass door and tried another, cautious smile, but Clare could see that he now plainly thought she was mad. She decided to go back to Lewis. And talk to Tony. On the way back down the corridor she imagined Tony softening, sharing a joke, a reminiscence, catching her roughly in an embarrassed embrace. But when she got back Tony had gone. Lewis' mother was sitting by the bed.
'Clare.'
She smelt of something undoubtedly expensive but which reminded Clare of a poodle parlour as she kissed the proffered cheek, wondering which of them was wincing the most. She knew Lewis' mother had never liked her. Lewis said himself that Raine held all his friends responsible for the moral downfall of her only son and Clare, being an artist, was high in the league of the dangerously

unconventional. There was a naivety to Raine's disappointment that was quite touching, her belief that if only Lewis had found decent friends, fallen in with the right crowd, then things would have been different. And perhaps now he would be married, and not famous for his risqué collection of unwearable clothes, and not lying in a hospital bed on a life support machine at the age of thirty.

'The doctor asked me . . . '

Raine opened her crocodile skin handbag and pulled out a white handkerchief.

'They need my permission to - to stop - '

She drew the handkerchief over her nose and mouth, and closed her eyes. Clare sat down next to her and took the other hand. It was dry and scaly with the eczema which covered most of her body. Clare resisted the urge to stroke the handbag, for comparison.

'I don't know what to do.'

Clare gripped the hand. Eventually Raine opened her eyes and removed the handkerchief. She sniffed and looked at Clare. Clare wondered whether or not to let go of her hand. She imagined Lewis looking at them in astonishment, delighted with the drama, and gently dropped it.

'So.'

Raine had a way of cultivating guilt with the smallest word.

'Do you know, Clare, if he had it? The disease. Do you know?'

Clare concentrated on her breathing.

'I don't know,' she said, 'and anyway, would it make any difference? Would it make it any easier?'

'Easier?'

'You know - reasons.'

She didn't add, as she wanted to, 'Gay men die of other things too.'

'Yes,' said Raine. 'Reasons.'

And suddenly Clare realised that was what she wanted to ask Lewis most of all. He'd left no note, and they said, by the amount of barbiturates and alcohol in his bloodstream when they hauled him out of the Thames, that he must have been serious. He was already, by that time, in an irreversible coma.

'Why didn't you tell me?' asked Raine. 'I'm his mother. You could have told me.'

Clare looked at her.

'Told you what?' she thought. 'Told you that you own son was always unhappy?'

Silently she took Raine's little scaly hand in her own. This was the woman who had given Lewis the gift of life, and he hadn't liked it. He had spat it back in her face. Clare slowed her breathing once more in rhythm with the ventilator.

Clunk. Ssss. Clunk. Ssss.

He was not quite dead. That was Raine's decision now, and in the meantime the two women sat together, waiting for Lewis to wake up.

Walking

Walking is good for you. If you ask me the world would be a much better place if everyone walked everywhere. There would be no wars for a start. If all the politicians and kings and queens and presidents had to travel by foot they would be far too tired to start arguing with each other.

It's a long walk from my hospital ward to the nearest café. Seven miles, someone told me once. Fourteen there and back. They built the hospital just far enough from London to keep all the loonies out of sight. It's an imposing Victorian building, standing dark and austere in lush grounds big enough to be, for many, an entire world. The enormous iron gates at the end of the long drive are always open now, but no-one bothers or dares to pass beyond. Remember when they thought the world was flat? If you went to the edge you would drop off. Fat Stella and one or two of the young men sit at the entrance all day long watching the cars. Fat Stella cries all the time, loud, snotty sobs. Few people pass the hospital on foot and the ones who do quicken their pace at the gates and pull their coats tightly around them. You can hear their thoughts, there but for the grace of God. They look at Fat Stella not with pity but with fear. The rest of the patients slump on the benches in the garden, lie stiffly on the grass, or shuffle round and round the little pathways that lead to nowhere, but you never see anyone leave. Except me, that is.

Today I button up the balding beaver collar of my mauve coat and nod at the gardener as I walk briskly up the drive, through the gates and on to the main road into London. I walk like a young woman. Everyone says so.
('Look at Mary - eighty-five you know, isn't she marvellous!')
One of the doctors told me I was a walking miracle, but I informed him that it was nothing to do with thaumaturgy, it was merely a matter of practise. It's a cold November day and beginning to spit with rain, but only my hands register the temperature. I watch them as they begin to turn blue, and then white.
'Put your gloves on, Mary,' George the nurse tells me as I am leaving,

although he knows I will return with my gloves still in the pockets of my coat. Tonight he will reach for my numb hands, playfully admonishing me in his Irish lilt as he rubs them between his own.

The rush hour traffic is slow and I cross the dual-carriageway, weaving between the bonnets of crawling motor cars. With a raised hand I indicate for a large Ford to stop and the driver, in irritation, presses his horn and mouths angrily at me. I stop directly in front of his bonnet and fix him with a severe stare. My eyes have always been my best feature, so I'm told.

('Look at Mary's eyes - have you ever seen eyes so blue?')

('Jesus, Mary, don't look at me like that - you give me the creeps!')

The driver tries some ineffective gesticulation and then winds down his window.

'For Christ's sake get a move on will you!'

I do not move.

'You stupid old cow - why can't you use the crossing like everyone else?'

Slowly I raise my arm higher and point my index finger directly between his eyes. It never fails. Just a glimmer, the merest gulp in his neck, before he winds up the window and begins repeatedly pumping the horn, but it is enough. I raise my eyebrows and pass through the traffic to the big housing estate on the other side of the road. Down the hill, past the station, a school playground full of brown children, and a church with a sign saying, 'Repent Now'. There are few people walking today. An angry mother pushing her pram and dragging a toddler by the arm. Two boys in school uniform running through the rain, laughing. As I reach the parade of shops I slow, pausing to take a look in the windows, but not for long. I am hungry.

One does not enjoy hospital food. The tea comes out of a giant metal pot, with a suspicious white scum on top which disappears before the half-wits notice, and all the food smells of fish. I suppose they think everyone is too mad to care. So I have my breakfast at The Star Kebab House where the owner, George, gives me tea in a cup and saucer and fetches me a bun or a jam tart from the bakers next door. Today he is standing, as usual, in the doorway of the dark little café and he waves and smiles, beckoning me in.

'Hello old Mary - how's my Mary?'

I object to his choice of adjective but then George is Turkish and they do things differently. Sometimes he sits with me at the little Formica table by the door and tells me stories about Turkey, showing me photographs of his children. He has told me his name many times, but I always call him George. I call all men George.

Wrapping my hands around the hot teacup I wait for George to fetch me my cake. He is frying chips for the schoolgirl with the very black hair and the very white face. Her eyes are pencilled dark in an attempt at adult sensuality but she looks like a small kitten, arching against the counter as she waits for her greasy bag of comfort. I have never seen George make a kebab. Although there is a long menu of different foreign dishes I've only ever seen him serve chips. The chips spit and a radio crackles and the girl moves her shoulders to the faintly discernible beat.

'There you go, my darling, careful now, they're hot.'

The girl counts out her change and saunters out, picking at the chips to avoid my gaze, as most young girls do. Who really wants to believe that one day they too will be old? George wipes his hands on his apron.

'Okay, old Mary, what's it to be? I get you something nice, eh?'

Quickly he slips out of the café and returns with a currant bun in a paper bag.

'Okay for you? You want butter?'

I tell him I would like a plate and a knife too.

These days the buns are different. Bread too. Everything is too light, insubstantial. They put too much air in everything these days. When I was young my mother baked every morning, bread rolls, pies, rock buns, heavy dough that you could feel inside you. I used to sit at the kitchen table making little figures out of the pastry cuttings, and my mother would let me bake the small effigies and eat them one by one. Heads first. She always said I was a strange little girl. After my father was killed in France my mother became deeply religious and took me to church every evening to pray for the destruction of the Huns, whom she regarded as the devil's own army. When the air raids started, she looked on with contempt as our neighbours scurried down the underground station like rabbits while she, proud and defiant, climbed on to the roof of our house to shout the wrath of God at the Zeppelins overhead. One evening, as we returned from church through the rubble of a raid, we passed a large hole in the ground, a six foot crater. At its edge I could see the legs of a man, sticking up as though he were diving into a pool. When I think of it now I swear his feet were kicking, but that could hardly have been possible. My mother raised her face to the heavens, called out to the Almighty, and then grabbed my hand and pulled me away, covering my eyes. But not before I had peered into the hole and seen the man with no head. My mother always said I was never the same again. Today, if you look through my fat hospital file you will find numerous references to the incident. Doctors love cause and effect. Often a keen student nurse will ask me gently and earnestly about my experiences of the war. But what I never tell them is that I was not in the least surprised by that body. I thought about it often, certainly, and my pastry people never had heads after that. I used to cut jagged necks with a knife and paint the edges with cochineal. But really, when I looked down into that hole, it was as if I had always known it would be there. For everyone, everywhere, there is a headless corpse just waiting round the corner. But I suppose most people never see it. Most people spend their lives looking the other way.

I finish my tea and take my cup to the sink behind the counter where George lets me wash up. I rinse it, as usual, twenty times, filling it to the brim, pouring water down the sink until George takes it from me. 'You English! Wasting water all the time. Give it here old Mary!'
I always wash my cup. It seems only right as I have no money to pay for the tea. As I dry my hands a man comes into the café and seats himself at my table.
'Sausage, egg, chips - thanks,' he calls before burying his head in a newspaper. I return to my seat, knocking the man's foot just slightly as I pull out my chair, and I see him glance from the side of his paper at my legs. He registers interest. I have good legs. Walking is good for the legs, and the young nurses say they would sell their souls for a pair like mine. In an instant the man's watery blue eyes have perused my entire body and come to rest, momentarily in horror, on my eighty-five year-old face, before returning to the more succulent

delights of the Sun. I ask him sweetly for a cigarette and, irritated, he reaches into his pocket without meeting my eyes. After such a blunder his guilty embarrassment makes him an easy touch and, were I in the habit of asking for money, I would be sure to make a small killing. I thank him for the cigarette and he passes me a box of matches, not bothering to tell me that his name isn't George. He has told himself that he would not touch me, not in a million years. But, as our eyes meet, we both know he would, if there was no-one else. No-one else to choose from and no-one else to see him do it. They do it to old ladies like me. To children too and even, sometimes, to sheep.

George was my first. My mother was pleased that I had a sweetheart, for she thought I was spending far too much time in my bedroom cutting pictures for my scrapbook. I collected pictures of people out of old books, any people I could find. Ladies in beautiful ballgowns, beggars, priests and judges and tiny children in ruffles and lace. Of course I cut all their heads off before pasting them into my book, and I joined their hands together to make a long, dancing line. My mother called it morbid, and so she was delighted when George, the grocer's son, began calling in the summer evenings to take me walking. Walking, however, was not all George had in mind.

It was only curiosity, but my mother was fond of telling me what that did to the cat. After George there were many others, for it was so easy to skip choir practice and walk on my own to the park, swinging my long plaits. There, behind the bushes, on the warm evenings of war, I learned how life was made. It seemed such a simple act, so simple that I was sure at first that there must be more. If death could be so varied, so enormously and expensively planned, then I was convinced that there must be more to the secret of creation than such a clumsy little manoeuvre. So I tried them all, city gents, soldiers, rich and poor, young and old, until I realised, watching each final grunt at my breast, that they all did exactly the same. As I said, it was only curiosity, but my mother had another word for it, and so did the doctors to whom she finally took me.

After they took the baby away I was locked in a bare white room. There were no windows and so I had to draw my headless companions on the white walls. I painted them in the cold, gelatinous gravy of my dinners, more successfully in the thicker textures of my slop bucket and finally, when I learned to bite the ends off my fingers, in blood.

My mother did not visit me. My only visitors were the nurses with the enormous evil-smelling syringe. There was one nurse to hold my arms, one to hold my legs, and one to jab a needle in my arse. I was held in cold baths, wrapped in freezing, wet towels, strapped to a metal bed and fed through a rubber tube. When my mother wrote she talked of my freedom, like a carrot, but as the days turned into weeks and months I felt myself more free than ever before. There is a peculiar kind of freedom in a cell. The freedom to kick and shit and spit. The freedom to scream.

And, do you know, you can walk just as far in a cell as anywhere in the world. Three and a half paces, turn, three and a half paces back. It adds up. They thought it was the injections that made me quiet and, years later, the electric shocks. But I know I have always walked myself into silence. When I stopped talking altogether they gave me more shocks to bring back the words that I'd trampled underfoot, and finally they drilled a hole in my head, thinking they could find my voice there. Then they let me out of the cell and I began to walk up and down the long white corridor, through the days and nights, days and years. I never saw my mother again. She sent me cards with pictures of Jesus and his disciples, and wrote to me of the cancer that was eating her bones.
'You did this to me, Mary,' she wrote when she was dying. 'You did this - you and the Huns.'

It's just stopped raining when I leave the café, waving goodbye to George.
'Take care now, Mary,' he tells me. 'Be good, Mary.'
That's what they all tell me, to be good. And mostly, these days, I am. Mostly now I am a sweet old lady in a fur-trimmed coat, a familiar figure on this route through the northern outskirts of London. A most suitable candidate, you might say, for community care.

That's what they call it, the hospital closing down. They come in hordes now, these new ones, shivering down the long corridor which they call an architectural marvel. They visit us in the wards, and talk of preparation and of freedom, wearing uniforms of blue jeans and earrings, the men too. They like to tell me they understand. The painting woman wears lots of silk scarves and her blackened eyes are smug with secrets. We sit around a table with poster paints and sheets of sugar paper and she looks at my little headless figures with a grave pleasure. Fat Stella sometimes comes and paints too but she never finishes her picture once she starts crying. The painting woman seems to like this; she holds Stella's hand and tells her she's doing well. When Stella's sobs begin the painting woman looks at her with pride, like she's hit the jackpot.

And then George comes to teach me how to cook. George, with his ponytail and his girl's voice who is young enough to be my grandson, comes to teach me how to live outside, in the pristine flats which they tell us will be our new homes. I like going to the supermarket. George lets me choose our lunch, and he enjoys explaining to me the value of the coins and notes. The ladies on the till call me 'love' and 'dear' and they nod and smile at George, telling him what a marvellous job he's doing. Usually I compliment George on the way back to the hospital, knowing that a bit of flattery will mean that he lets me sit with a cup of tea while he makes the lunch. It was George who took me to see the little box where they think I will live. I told him straight away that I would not go, that the hospital had suited me well enough for seventy years, but George patted my hand and told me that even the most wonderful opportunities took some getting used to. He told me I would do well on the outside, that my community orientation was already perfect and my social skills almost impeccable. He said they would all be proud of me.

As I step into the wet street outside the café I see the brick. It's lying beneath the scaffolding surrounding the newsagents. Really it is only half a brick, but it will do. No-one bothers about the old lady stooping under the scaffolding to pick it up and so I have time to perfect my position in front of The Star Kebab house and take aim. My arms are nearly as strong as my legs. There is an explosion of shattering glass and suddenly everyone around me notices that I exist. George is running to his broken window, waving his arms. George is staring at the glass in his dinner, blood trickling from a splinter in his cheek. Georges everywhere stop and look at me as I wait for the sirens.

The two policemen are surprised to see their culprit. I tell them my full name and give the address of the hospital, which makes them nod at each other. One of them starts talking into his radio while the other ushers me firmly into the car.

'Shouldn't let them out really,' he mutters to his partner. He grins at me, a boy's nervous grin.

'Right then, love, let's get you back.'

I give him my sweetest smile and he looks relieved. Sometimes I enjoy a ride in a police car, and it looks impressive in my hospital file. Tonight George will sigh as he fills in his special report form.

'You've blown it again, Mary,' he will tell me, shaking his head. 'Now you're never going to get out of here.'

I'm rather looking forward to a month or two back on the locked ward. At this time of year it's always so dark and wet outside, and the locked ward has a nice stretch of blue carpet, thirty feet by ten, well worn. As I said, walking is good for you. It doesn't matter where you go.